Y0-BRV-523

Desirée Mays

Opera Unveiled

2000

♪

Illustrated
by
Karen H.-Fitzsimmons

Katydid Books
Santa Fe

KATYDID BOOKS

#1 Balsa Rd., Santa Fe, New Mexico 87505

Opera Unveiled 2000 copyright © 2000 by Katydid Books.
Text copyright © 2000 by Desirée Mays.
Cover art and illustrations copyright © 2000 by Karen Hargreaves-Fitzsimmons.

All rights reserved.
Except for short citations, no portion of this book may be reproduced
without the permission of both the author and the publisher.

Distributed by Art Forms, Inc., 31 Valencia Loop, Santa Fe, NM 87505
Fax (505) 466 1908

Produced by KT DID Productions.
Printed and bound in the United States of America on acid-free paper.

Back cover photograph by Carolyn Wright

First edition

Library of Congress Cataloging-in-Publication Data
Mays, Desirée
Opera Unveiled 2000 / by Desirée Mays. -- 1st ed.
p.   cm.
Includes bibliographical references.
Contents: Rigoletto / Giuseppe Verdi -- Le nozze di Figaro / Wolfgang Amadeus Mozart -- Elektra /
Richard Strauss -- Ermione / Gioacchino Rossini -- Venus and Adonis / Hans Werner Henze.
ISBN 0-942668-54-5
1. Opera. 1. Title: Opera unveiled two thousand. II. Title.
ML170O.M26 2000
782.1--dc2i
99-053616

CIP

To order further copies of *Opera Unveiled 2000*, please send a check made
out to Art Forms Inc. for $15 (postage paid)
to:
Art Forms Inc,. 31 Valencia Loop, Santa Fe, New Mexico 87505
Fax: (505) 466-1908

CONTENTS

to

Eleanor

INTRODUCTION

Hans Werner Henze, composer of *Venus and Adonis*, the opera which will have its American première at The Santa Fe Opera this season, said, "Art isn't about itself; it's about how people relate to the world and each other; it's one of the ways society creates its identity. It's not primitive and dark, but rational and constructive."* For Henze, the fundamental need to communicate is an essential part of human nature. This being the case, how do the five operas of the 2000 season of The Santa Fe Opera stack up?

The question is not so simple, for these five operas are based on five outstanding works of literature. *Rigoletto* is based on Victor Hugo's *Le Roi s'amuse*, *Le Nozze di Figaro* on Beaumarchais' play of the same name, *Elektra* on the Greek play by Sophocles, *Ermione* on a play by Racine, and *Venus and Adonis* on the Shakespearian poem. But maybe these five sources and five operas illustrate the point that art is about how society creates and communicates its identity.

Mozart and Verdi, in their two operas, *Le Nozze di Figaro* and *Rigoletto*, took on the systems of their days. Mozart, in the character of Figaro, confronts the old system, the *ancien régime*, where servants, women, and the young had few rights. The Count attempts to impose the ancient *droit de seigneur*, or the right of the first night, when the Lord seduces the bride of a servant on the wedding night. Figaro challenges the system - and wins. Napoleon called this opera "revolution in action." Though the French Revolution may be far behind us now in the 21st-century, Mozart fought the good fight for all in his day.

Verdi, nearly seventy years later, did the same thing in taking up the Hugo play and exposing the licentiousness of a king. Because of the content of their operas, Mozart and Verdi ran into trouble with the censors. Both found ways around this difficulty and their works were performed; the Queen of France, Marie

♪

* Edward Bond and Hans Werner Henze, "Notes on *We Come to the River*," The Santa Fe Opera Program, Summer 1984.

Antoinette, interceded on behalf of the Beaumarchais play, and the humanist Austrian Emperor Joseph II allowed performances to proceed after hearing Mozart's music. In the case of Verdi, a little expeditious manipulation by Piave, his censor-wise librettist, allowed *Rigoletto* to see the light of day. Beaumarchais, Mozart, Hugo, and Verdi spoke up and challenged their societies.

Henze continues, "We create in order to listen, just as men use words in order to listen. The artist relates his ego to society in a way that enables his audience to recognize a common, shared humanity." This is true of all the operas. As Mozart and Verdi focus on the place of man in his society, Strauss and Rossini focus, in *Elektra* and *Ermione,* on the passions that rule our actions. Both operas, coincidentally, explore the passions of the same family who are enshrined in Greek myth. The treatments of the two operas are very different. Rossini, composing in 1819, uses the style of *opera seria*, while Strauss, in 1909, composes in a 20th-century style of post-romanticism. While styles, sets, and costumes change over time, the essential passions described in the two operas are timeless. *Elektra* describes the bloody process whereby the outraged daughter of Agamemnon, dreaming only of vengeance, sacrifices all else to her purpose — the death of her mother and stepfather in retribution for her father's murder. Rossini deals with a more intimate drama: the furious Ermione, who, torn between love and hate, destroys the man she loves. We can listen and learn from this: from Elektra, whose actions change the direction of a whole society; and from Ermione, whose obsessive passion causes devastation on a smaller scale.

Henze believes that art is about realism: "Art is realism or it is trivial, there is nothing much in between." Though some of these operas may be cloaked in the mists of distant pasts, each is relevant and realistic. The trauma involved in the eternal love triangle, as in Henze's own opera, *Venus and Adonis*, has not changed since the time of Shakespeare, whose poem was the source of the opera. Rigoletto is all too believable as the clown who must hide a broken heart when his daughter is ravished by his boss. Mozart's Countess suffers when her husband pursues younger women. Ermione has the man who spurned her killed. Musical styles and time periods are almost irrelevant in terms of what is going on in the story; the human drama is as meaningful now as then. We can listen and learn from opera's depiction of issues that are far from trivial.

Since opera is perceived by many as dealing mainly with tragedy, trauma, angst, and death, Henze says, surprisingly, "Art is always optimistic and rational." Opera, he believes, explores human relationships, "destroying cloaks of sentimentality, hypocrisy, and myth." Mozart seriously considers the state of marriage in *Le Nozze di Figaro* with an optimism and a compassion that are astonishing. *Elektra* goes straight for the jugular, both in the story and in Strauss's music — we cannot stay outside of her pain or her madness. Yet, in some cathartic way, we understand and sympathize with her pain. In *Ermione,* rationality is restored when all the leading characters are destroyed and Andromaca, the captive Trojan princess who remains true to her fallen husband, assumes the throne in place of those who ruled by their passions.

In the early days of opera the subject matter focused exclusively on gods and kings. This has changed, for while "The opera house may seem remote from the street, the nature of art is controlled by the man in the street. Art turns to the street, marketplace, factory, or slum because this is where social relationships, shared responsibilities, are breaking down and have to be re-created." (Henze) *Verismo,* or realism in opera, was criticized because it dealt with these very situations in works such as *I Pagliacci, Carmen, Wozzeck,* and *Lulu.* Contemporary operas reflect our times, often in terms we may not want to accept or recognize. In Greek times (*Elektra* and *Ermione*) the battle was between royal families; for Beaumarchais and Mozart, just before the French Revolution, the struggle was for individual freedom and an end to royal right. In *Venus and Adonis*, in a sophisticated double layering of one plot by the same three characters, the struggles of a 20th- century relationship are tragically resolved.

The stories are told twice, once in the drama and once in the music. These five great composers are masters of orchestration. If we listen carefully we can often hear, in the music, that which is not stated in the words. That is the wonder of opera above any other art form: its ability to communicate with us through music, along with the story, sets, costumes, and lighting, all that is being expressed in the voices of the singers. We have only to listen.

La Maledizione

Rigoletto

Rigoletto, George Bernard Shaw pronounced, was "burned into music by Verdi." In the words of the composer, Giuseppe Verdi, the hunchbacked jester was "Outwardly ridiculous and deformed, inwardly filled with passion and love." *Rigoletto* is permanently etched, held, and heard in the glorious melodies of Verdi's opera.

Verdi wrote to his librettist, Francesco Maria Piave, in 1850, that he sought a text for his new opera that was "grandiose, passionate, fantastic," and believed he had found a subject in a "character that is one of the greatest creations the theatre can boast of. The subject is *Le Roi s'amuse.*" This powerful and controversial drama about a hunchbacked jester had been written as a play by Victor Hugo in 1832. Verdi was quick to see that the play read like an opera. The story line was strong and direct, while the larger-than-life characters of The King (The Duke in the opera), the hunchback Triboulet (Rigoletto), and Blanche (Gilda) had enormous appeal.

Hugo's play is set at a lavish party in the Louvre, which served as the 16th-century palace of King François I of France. The assembly glitters in the ornate Renaissance costumes of the day. The King, a handsome, virile man, is talking with a friend about a young woman "of rank obscure, her very name concealed" whom he saw at church and wants to get to know. He is somewhat mystified by "the strange, unearthly form, whose features night conceals, enshrouded close in mantle dark," who visits the young woman each night. But the King is soon distracted by the wife of a courtier, Madame De Cossé (Countess Ceprano in the opera), and flirts with her. Triboulet enters — the clown, the jester, the hunchbacked but agile fool with bells on his cap, a jester's bauble in his hand. When the King demands if the court poet, Marot, has his verses of love ready, Hugo has a little joke at the expense of poets, "Make love, O Sire," Triboulet replies, "and let Marot make verse, it but degrades a king." The King and Triboulet banter back and forth discussing the courtiers, who are angered by the jester's cutting flippancy. Triboulet eggs the King on and suggests he take De Cossé's wife while sending her husband to the Bastille, banishment, or, "One method, simple and concise, cut off his head." The courtiers laugh nervously while De Cossé furiously confronts the Fool.

The courtiers believe that Triboulet has a mistress whom he visits every night. This causes much merriment, then takes on a serious tone as the offended De Cossé suggests they kidnap Triboulet's mistress that very night so as to be revenged on the Fool. The flirtation and plot-making cease as a voice is heard offstage: "I'll see the King." It is Monsieur de St. Vallier (Count Monterone in the opera), whose daughter has been abducted and dishonored by the King. St. Vallier insists, "You, François of Valois, without one spark of love or pity or remorse, did on that night with cold embraces, foully bring scorn on my helpless daughter." The King, angered, orders his arrest while Triboulet makes fun of him. St. Vallier curses the King and his jester, "Oh, Sire! 'tis wrong upon the dying lion to loose thy dog," and then, directly to Triboulet, "And thou that with a fiendish sneer and viper's tongue makest my tears a pastime and a sport, My curse on thee." ("*Sii maledetto!*"). With this terrible curse, the first scene ends in play and opera alike.

Later that afternoon Triboulet makes his way home, enveloped in a cloak and muttering to himself, "The old man cursed me." As he nears a house surrounded by a high wall, he is approached by a dark man. Triboulet tries to brush him off, but the man, Saltabadil (Sparafucile in the opera), tells him he has come to offer his services "By my good sword I live. By this hand he dies." He is an assassin. Triboulet inquires the price to slay a noblemen and the two men discuss terms. Saltabadil explains how his sister entices men to his inn, where they are neatly dispatched for a price. He tells Triboulet where he may be found and leaves. Triboulet watches him go and ponders, "How much alike his cruel trade to mine; His sword is sharp, but with a tongue more keen I stab the heart! Aye, deeper far than he."

Triboulet looks about him, then, seeing no one in the street, takes out a key and opens the door in the wall — for this is his home, the home he goes to extraordinary lengths to keep concealed, for it holds the person more dear to him than life: his daughter, Blanche (Gilda in the opera). Still haunted by the curse, in a long soliloquy the jester cries out against nature, which made him wicked, heartless, and depraved — a buffoon. He hates the young, handsome king who makes him act the fool. He pays back bitter sneers with scorn. He would destroy "The happiness of all, covering with hollow, false, malignant smile the venomed hate that festers at my heart."

His reverie is broken by his daughter, who runs to greet him *"Mio padre!" "Mia figlia!"* ("My father!" "My child!") Blanche is sixteen and innocent. Her life is sheltered; her father will allow her to go out only to mass on Sundays with her duenna, Berarde (Giovanna in the opera). Triboulet greets her rapturously. Blanche is concerned at his sorrow and gently asks, "Who are our friends, who is my mother?" Triboulet describes the woman who loved him in spite of his deformity and his wretchedness, the woman who died, leaving him Blanche. He sobs as Blanche comforts him and asks his name. "I am thy father. Ask me not for more. No name is holier than a father's to his child." He tells Blanche she is his universe and seems to confuse mother and daughter in the lines "My soul leaps forth to thine, even in darkness I can see thee still, for thou art day and light and life to me." He reminds Blanche she must not leave the house; he is terrified she will be abducted, "Pursued, torn from me, and disgraced. The wretched jester's daughter none would pity." He calls Dame Berarde to confirm that Blanche never goes out. Berarde reassures him. Triboulet goes to the gate and into the street to check. As he does so, the King, in disguise, slips into the garden and hides. Triboulet returns, and holds Blanche in his arms for a moment as he bids her farewell.

Left alone with Berarde, Blanche feels guilty at not having told her father about the young man who has been following her home from church. Berarde, standing near the hidden king, replies that the unknown stranger is charming, discreet, magnificent. At each of these adjectives the king puts money in the duenna's hand, unseen by Blanche. This can be a highly comic scene, lightening the growing tension of the story. Blanche declares her love for the young man who suddenly appears before her. Confused, she asks him to leave, but he woos and wins her with an ode to love. Blanche asks his name. "Godfrey Meleune, a student poor," he replies (Gaultier Maldè in the opera).

A disturbance is heard outside; the courtiers are gathering to abduct Blanche. The King, unaware of the plot, is angry at the interruption but must leave. Kissing Blanche passionately, he disappears into the night. Left alone, Blanche caresses his name, "Name that I adore." (This is the famous *"Caro nome"* aria in the opera.)

Outside, the men in the street are preparing to scale the wall with a ladder when Triboulet appears. They quickly tell him they plan to abduct De Cossé's wife from the building next to his. But, Triboulet is told, they must all wear masks to avoid being recognized. Laughing to themselves, they blindfold Triboulet and ask him to hold the ladder, which he does. The men mount the ladder, climb onto the terrace, and disappear inside the house. Moments later they reappear with the struggling Blanche and escape with her. She cries out to her father, who tears off the blindfold and realizes with horror that it is his beloved Blanche who has been abducted. His tears his hair, crying "The curse! The curse!" (*"La Maledizione!"*).

Early next morning, the scene is set in the royal antechamber in the Louvre. The courtiers are congratulating themselves on the success of the night's escapade and relishing the moment Triboulet will find out about the abduction of his mistress, "Let the slave, in agony and tears, pay in one day our long arrears of hate." The king is told of the plot and asks to see the girl. When Blanche enters, both are amazed — Blanche on recognizing that the poor student she loves is really the king, and the king in delight that his prey has been so easily captured.

The following scene appears in the play but was cut from the opera at the insistence of the censors, who labeled it as both obscene and immoral. The king tells Blanche he loves her, "We'll be two lovers wedded in delight. Blanche, wilt not be my Queen?" "The Queen! Your wife?" "The Queen, my mistress: 'tis a fairer name," replies the king. At last Blanche understands the truth. Horrified, she cries that her father will protect her. She runs to a nearby room as the king follows her, slams the door, and locks it behind him. Blanche was not to know the room was the king's bed-chamber. "The sheep seeks refuge in the lion's den," laugh the courtiers.

The opera returns to the plot at this point. Triboulet, dressed in his jester's clothes, walks around as the courtiers gossip in front of the door to the king's chamber. He knows the courtiers are guilty, but he does not know where they have hidden Blanche. He attempts to enter the king's bedroom but is barred. He finally cries out "Give me back my child!" The courtiers are surprised. The woman they abducted was not Triboulet's mistress but his daughter? Triboulet gives vent to his rage, lambasting the men and calling them bastards — another line the censor took exception to before banning the play. A mere servant could not malign his master in this manner on any stage in France.

Suddenly the door of the king's room opens and a disheveled Blanche comes running out. With a cry of terror, she throws herself into her father's arms. In this moment of terrible recognition for father and daughter, Blanche discovers the true nature of her father's work as the king's jester, while his worst fears are confirmed when he learns that his daughter has been deflowered by his king. Triboulet orders the courtiers from the room, "Get ye hence." Intimidated but still smirking, they leave.

Blanche now tells her father she was raped by the king, whom she believed to be a poor student. Triboulet swears vengeance to heaven just as St. Vallier appears and says that, since the king still lives, his curse must be in vain. In the last line of this tempestuous scene, Triboulet turns to him, and says, "Old man, 'tis false. There's one shall strike for thee."

The final act is set near the gates of Paris. The stage is divided in the center: on one side there is a darkened river path by the Seine; on the other, divided by a dilapidated wall, is a disreputable inn owned by Saltabadil. The lower room is wretchedly furnished. A narrow staircase at the back leads to a loft or attic. Saltabadil sits at a table cleaning his belt. Outside the wall, Triboulet appears with Blanche, who tells her father that she still loves the King. From the play it is clear, that in the intervening month, Blanche has settled down as the mistress of the king, but now Triboulet plans to show her the faithlessness of the man she loves. He draws her near the wall, and both stand motionless as they gaze through the chinks in the wall.

The king, dressed as an officer, enters. "Your sister and a glass," he demands of Saltabadil. While waiting, the king sings a famous dictum of the historical King François: "Women are frequently fickle, he who trusts them is mad" (*Souvent femme varie, bien fol est qui s'y fie!*). These lines inspired Verdi's *"La donna è mobile"* ("Woman is fickle as a feather in the breeze"). Blanche, watching from outside the wall, gasps as Maguelonne, (Maddalena), Saltabadil's sister, appears inside the house and flirts with the king. Saltabadil leaves the house for a moment to ask Triboulet, "Shall he die now?" "Not yet." The king, led on by the flirtatious Maguelonne, says, "I'll marry thee." This is too much for Blanche. "What thinkest thou now of vengeance?" Triboulet asks. "Do as thou wilt," she replies. He tells her to leave, to go home, disguise herself as a man, and leave Paris. He will join her the following day. Blanche leaves in despair.

Saltabadil once more appears at Triboulet's side. The jester hands over half the money, saying he will return at midnight for the body. Saltabadil agrees: "It shall be done. What is the name of this gallant?" In a voice of anguish and despair Triboulet replies, "His name is Crime, and mine Punishment." (*"Il s'appelle le crime, et moi le chatiment."* — Hugo. *"Egli è Delitto, Punizion son io"* — Verdi.) It is a dark, wild night; a storm starts to build as the king mounts the stairs to the attic and retires for the night. Maguelonne, who has taken a fancy to the young officer, suggests to her brother that they kill the hunchback in place of the officer. Saltabadil responds indignantly, "I'll hear no more of this. Am I a thief, a bandit, cut-throat, cheat? Woulds't have me rob the client who employs and pays my sword?" But he agrees to compromise. If a stranger should knock at the inn before midnight, the stranger will be stabbed and given to Triboulet in the officer's place.

Blanche, dressed as a man and unable to stay away, returns in time to hear this last exchange. "Oh God! Thou temptest me! Thou bid'st me die to save a perjured life!" She agonizes in her love for the king and the idea of dying in his place. Finally she summons up her courage and knocks weakly at the door in the pouring rain. Saltabadil and his sister call out, "Who's there?" "A weary traveler." The murderers confer quickly and then, as Maguelonne opens wide the door, Blanche crosses the threshold and Saltabadil strikes.

Moments later all is still, the storm gradually subsides. The door to the inn is closed and dark. Triboulet returns triumphant, "Mysterious night, in heaven a tempest; murder on earth. Now am I great indeed. I've slain a King!" At the stroke of midnight the door opens and Saltabadil comes out dragging a sack — the sack that holds the victim. He offers to help Triboulet throw it in the Seine, but Triboulet says, "Alone I'll do it." He hands over the gold and Saltabadil returns to his house. Triboulet gloats over the sack, putting his foot on the body, "The Fool becomes the executioner of kings!" He starts to drag the sack toward the river when a sound from the inn stops him, the sound of the king singing — "Women are fickle." Triboulet believes he has heard a ghost, then turns in horror to the sack. If the king lives, then who died? He opens the sack and in the brightness of a lightning flash the face of Blanche is revealed. He has been tricked! Triboulet is distraught. Blanche, dying, her shirt covered in blood, her hair loose, calls to her father, "'Tis for him I die." She struggles for breath, and her head falls on her father's shoulder. Triboulet cries out for help. Passersby gather around father and daughter. Triboulet, in his grief, holds Blanche, imagining her alive, a child once more. "Now she sleeps," he says as a surgeon enters and, taking Blanche's pulse, pronounces her dead. Triboulet collapses with a final, soul-searing cry of pain: "I have slain my child."

Verdi and Piave chose a slightly different but more effective ending for the opera's final moments. Rigoletto and Gilda remain alone on stage as Gilda sings, "Soon, in Heaven, when I am near to my mother, in eternity I'll pray for you." As she dies, Rigoletto cries out, "Gilda, my Gilda, she's dead!" (*"La Maledizione!"*) as the curtain falls.

This is the story of the play by Victor Hugo, the play that was so closely followed in the operatic version by Verdi and Piave. The thirty-year-old Victor Hugo had become sensationally successful in Paris with his historical drama, *Hernani*, the same *Hernani* from which Verdi composed his opera, *Ernani*, in 1844. The French play broke all the rules of French theatre and scandalized audiences, but it made Hugo famous.

Le Roi s'amuse was commissioned by the Théâtre Français in 1832. Hugo had given much thought to the character of the hunchback, for he was fascinated by the wisdom of Shakespeare's Fools and by the character of Quasimodo in *Notre Dame de Paris*.

Hugo based the character of Triboulet on the real jester at the 16th-century court of François I.

Though censorship was officially abolished in France following the revolution of 1830, Hugo was aware there might be difficulties with *Le Roi s'amuse*. He was not, however, prepared for the near-riot that greeted the first, and only, night of *Le Roi s'amuse* on November 24. Catcalls, hissing, and booing assailed the performers. Was Hugo suggesting regicide when Triboulet rails against the courtiers, "Your mothers all prostituted themselves to lackeys. You are all bastards!" The play was clearly subversive, democratic, and revolutionary. In the Théâtre Français, a high temple of French art, the aristocracy could not be seen to behave this way. Kings could not run amok in brothels and seduce commoners. The reviews were damning. The final straw came with a message from the government banning all further performances of the play.

Hugo was furious, "Today I am gagged; tomorrow I shall be transported." He published the play at once and defended himself in the Preface. He attacks the Ministry on grounds of the illegality of censorship, then takes up the issue of morality. "The piece is immoral? Is it from its subject? Triboulet is deformed, unhealthy, a court buffoon — a threefold misery which renders him evil?" St. Vallier's curse on Triboulet, Hugo argues, is the real subject of the drama, for the curse falls on Triboulet, the father of a beloved daughter. Everything transpires against Triboulet. The king ravishes his daughter; the trap he lays for the king is the one into which his daughter falls and dies. Wishing to kill the king, he kills his daughter. The punishment of Triboulet is total, so where is the immorality?

Clearly, *Le Roi s'amuse* was red-hot material politically, but Italy was a long way from Paris in the mid-1800s. When Verdi read the play, he wrote to his librettist, "*Le Roi s'amuse* is the greatest plot, perhaps the greatest drama of modern times.

Triboulet is a creation worthy of Shakespeare. After reviewing several subjects, like a bolt of lightning, like an inspiration, I thought of *Le Roi s'amuse*. Turn Venice upside down to make the censors permit this subject." Censorship in Italy was an erratic affair in Verdi's day. Small Italian kingdoms and duchies each had their own set of rules concerning censorship, each dictated by very different political ideologies. Three taboo subjects, however, were common to all: politics, religion, and morality.

Piave, more aware than Verdi of the potential censorship problems, was concerned. The play depicted a royal king whose palace was a hotbed of debauchery and corruption in a story with a curse, a seduction, an assassination, and was peopled by a corrupt king, a hunchback jester, a professional assassin, and his prostitute sister. Nor did the king's violation of Blanche and the body in the sack at the end, bode well. It did not matter that the real king of France had been the model for the play. Verdi was at first concerned and angry to hear of the difficulties, and later he was furious when he heard that the Public Order Office in Venice absolutely refused to allow any opera based on the play to be performed. Piave went into action. The usual way around the censor was to change the time and the place of the story and the names of the characters. The first compromise along these lines was unacceptable to Verdi. Further negotiations brought results: The setting had to be changed from the French court to the court of a minor absolutist Italian state. The original characters could be retained, but the names must be changed. The bedroom scene between the king and Blanche must be excluded. The sack could stay in.

So the setting was moved from France to Italy; the real French King became the fictitious Duke of Mantua. The time period remained the 16th century. All the characters were renamed until, after months of work and negotiation with the censors, Piave was able to write to Verdi, *"Te deum laudamus! Gloria in excelsis*

Deo! Alleluja! Alleluja!" The final libretto had passed the test and was delivered to the directors of the theatre. "Finally our *Rigoletto* has returned, safe and sound, without fractures or amputations," Piave reported.

The title of the work underwent many changes in the course of these busy months in 1850-51. Verdi favored *Triboletto*, after the French. *La Maledizione* ("The Curse") became the working title, but finally Verdi and Piave settled on *Rigoletto*, a name derived from the French verb *rigoler*, to guffaw. This, however, was not quite the end of the line in terms of titles, for in order to get round various local censors, *Rigoletto* has appeared as *Clara di Perth, Viscardello,* and *Lionello.*

Rigoletto, the hunchbacked jester, would seem to be an odd choice of character to place at the center of a play or opera, yet the image of the court jester came from a long tradition of court fools in both history and literature. Professional jesters had been employed by the rich and powerful from ancient Egyptian times to the 18th century. Crazy or deformed people were typically seen as a source of amusement. The Fool was treated with great effect by Shakespeare. In madness or innocence, whether real or pretended, Shakespeare's Fools could mock the pretensions of the court. The costume of the jester, like the dress of clowns today, pokes fun at the customs of society. Shakespearian Fools take advantage of their immunity, and their position close to the seat of power, to comment on unwelcome or comic truths. Hugo's Triboulet is an example of the duality of personality that theatre explores so well. The stunted frame of the man in a servile and demeaning profession contrasts sharply with the love of a father for his daughter in private life. Triboulet's humor may be cynical, cutting but not witty, his hatred malignant, and his biting tongue rabid, but his love for his daughter is all-encompassing.

The powerless rage of the misshapen hunchback made the court laugh, yet his disfigured features make him vulnerable and touching. In the traditional manner of the clown, Rigoletto combines tragedy and comedy within himself, joyful as he sings of revenge, heartbroken as he sings of loss. He is a victim of farce, this Fool who, blindfolded, laughs unsuspectingly as his daughter is abducted. Here is a jester who fears laughter, whose bitterness has eaten away his soul.

The moment of recognition in the second act, when Gilda runs to him from the Duke's room, is doubly devastating for Rigoletto. He is haunted by the curse of Monterone, referring to it four times in the second act, and ending Acts 1 and 3 with *"La Maledizione!"* Verdi believed, like Hugo, that the opera was a working out of the curse. Monterone, a father, curses another father, Rigoletto, and, in cursing him, condemns the jester's daughter to death.

The first Rigoletto, Varesi, a baritone beloved by Verdi, had misgivings about appearing on stage as a buffoon. His daughter describes his first entrance: "My father, ashamed and timid in his ridiculous buffoon's costume, did not know how to pluck up courage to appear before the public, for he feared their derision. At the last moment it was Verdi himself who, giving him a shove to get on stage, made him stumble over the boards and flung him on stage, staggering all over the place. The audience was enraptured."

The libertine Duke of Mantua is reminiscent of Mozart's Don Giovanni. His first aria, delivered within minutes of his first entrance, is *"Questa o quella"* ("This woman or that, to me they're just the same"). Rigoletto describes him as "happy, influential, attractive, handsome," and hates him on all these counts; the Duke is everything Rigoletto is not. There is an echo of *Don Giovanni* in the relationship of the Duke and his jester with Don Giovanni and Leporello; both servants act as procurers for their dissolute masters, and both laugh at the misery they cause others. The minuet at the start of *Rigoletto* could have come straight from the ball in *Don Giovanni*, where Leporello/Rigoletto try to set up assignations for their masters with the women those masters desire.

The Duke makes love to two women in the opera: the purest girl in Mantua, and a prostitute in a disreputable inn. Musically, the means of seduction for both women is more or less the same: this man does not discriminate. The Duke, who is a master of disguise, suggests that Rigoletto is not alone in the wearing of a mask. With Gilda the Duke feigns to be a student and, like a character actor, falls into the role of a student madly in love with a young, innocent woman. When he discovers his new love presented to him on a plate, so to speak, in his own bedroom, his tone changes. Now he will seduce Gilda whether she wants him or not. If the girl will not take his hand and come willingly (more echoes of Giovanni's *"La cì darem la mano"*), then rape is another option to satisfy his desire.

This said, it is hard to be totally convinced that the Duke is evil through and through; this is partly Verdi's fault, for he composes the loveliest music for his promiscuous Duke. Does he love Gilda or not? Or is she only attractive to him momentarily because she is unattainable? Once conquered, will she be forgotten and abandoned? That is exactly what happens, for, a month after her abduction, the Duke is found carousing with Sparafucile's sister at the inn. The character of the Duke must be freshly defined each time he is played, depending on how the director and the tenor choose to interpret this philistine prince.

Gilda is sixteen years of age, sheltered, and with all the natural longings of a young girl in love with love. She falls easily for the good-looking student who follows her home from church. When he appears in her courtyard, aided and abetted by her duenna, she doesn't turn him away. Following her abduction, however, she is deeply changed. Forced into intimacy with the Duke, she finds that she still loves him and believes he loves her. When her father shows her the truth of the Duke's infidelity, and when she hears for herself the very same words of love the Duke sang to her, only then does she turn against him. Her change of heart is only temporary, for when she returns to Sparafucile's inn, she doesn't hesitate to take the place of the Duke and die for him. She will die for love, as so many operatic heroines have done before her and will continue to do. This is a role for a coloratura soprano, but the innocent Gilda displays little of the sophistication a coloratura role would imply. Her soaring *"Caro nome"* with its embellishments tells only of a young girl's happiness in the joy of her first love.

Sparafucile, a bass in every sense of the word, is an extraordinary invention in the play and opera. Offering Rigoletto the means whereby he can dispose of the Duke, Sparafucile, a businessman, calmly and clearly describes his method of killing. In an unexpected turn of character at the inn, he refuses to kill Rigoletto instead of the Duke. Maddalena, his sister, has no such compunctions. Kill him, she says, so I can have the handsome stranger. Maddalena flirts with the Duke, but is under no illusion as to what he wants of her. She is attracted to him but doesn't fall for him, as Gilda did.

These five are the leading characters. Count Monterone, a baritone, must be strongly played even though his role is small, for it is he, father of a disgraced daughter, who administers the curse that drives the plot.

Verdi composed *Rigoletto* during the years generally referred to as his second or middle period, following his "galley" years, *"anni di galera,"* as he called them himself. The great nationalistic operas, *Nabucco, Ernani, Attila,* and *Giovanna d'Arco* behind him, he now composed three extraordinary operas in the space of three years: *Rigoletto* in 1851, and *Il Trovatore* and *La Traviata* in 1853. Eminently successful at this time in his career, he was commissioned by Teatro la Fenice in Venice for a new opera in 1850. He had already collaborated with Piave on five operas, including *Ernani, Macbeth*, and *Stiffelio.* Following the long months of dispute with the censor, the first night of *Rigoletto,* held at La Fenice in March 1851 was a success. Reviews following the first night ranged from "The instrumentation is stupendous, admirable; the orchestra speaks to you, cries out to you; it instills passion in you. There was never such powerful eloquence in sound" (*Gazzetta Previlegiata di Venezia*) to "Monstrous, indecent, horrifying, and a veritable textbook of crime."

The melodies in this opera are truly remarkable; they flow from Verdi's pen one after another in waves of unforgettable sound. In *Rigoletto*, Verdi moved away from the traditional Italian operatic style and its conventions. He said, "I conceived *Rigoletto* without arias, without finales, as an unbroken chain of duets, because I was convinced that was the most suitable." The older structure still underlies the score, but it is flexible. Verdi allows the arias and duets to rise out of the dramatic action, not the other way around. With *Rigoletto*, one begins to realize the extraordinary depth of psychological insight with which Verdi probes and presents his characters.

The very opening bars of the overture plunge us into the mood of the action, as the sound of Monterone's Curse rings forth in solemn tones from the brass. Then, as the curtain opens, that theme is put away as a *banda*, a stage band, presents a series of dance tunes in an anachronistic, superficial style. The Duke sings of his flirtations to the accompaniment of an aristocratic *minuet* and a *perigordine*, a French country dance in 6/8 time.

The Duke launches into his first catchy *ballata*, *"Questa o quella"* ("Every woman is lovely"), early in the first scene, airing his shallow philosophy of love in this dance song, again in the French style. His famous aria of the last act, *"La donna è mobile,"* expresses similar sentiments. Verdi, perhaps sensing how popular this brief song would become, did not reveal it until the day of the dress rehearsal, when he finally handed it to the tenor.

The Duke is, in some ways, an ambiguous character; he is cynical one moment, and expresses all the passion of a *bel canto* romantic idealist the next. To Gilda he sings *"È il sol dell'anima"*

("Love is the source of life") to a gloriously flowing, lyrical melody. He expresses the same sentiments along the same lines to Maddalena in the inn. His *"Bella figlia dell'amore"* ("Beautiful child of love"), which starts the famous quartet, is as passionate and heartfelt as any music he sang to Gilda.

Gilda has but one, very beautiful, reverie-like song, *"Caro nome"* ("Dearest name"). This song is composed in one movement, as Verdi begins to change the structure of set arias. Two flutes and a violin punctuate the musical thoughts of this young girl responding to the first declarations of love.

Rigoletto's soliloquies are *ariosi* — that is, a mix of recitative and aria — which allows the flexibility of dialogue to combine with the emotional outpouring of the aria form. His *"Pari siamo"* in which he compares himself to Sparafucile, is an *arioso*. His second-act *arioso*, *"Cortigiani, vil razzo"* ("Courtiers, you vile, damned race"), is in three sections or movements, starting with the ungainly, meaningless melody of the buffoon, *"La-rà, la-rà, la-rà,"* as he enters pretending to play the jester while seeking his daughter. His rising fury is then described relentlessly in the strings as he attacks the courtiers; and finally, in the last section, the cello and cor anglais double the vocal line as Rigoletto pathetically entreats the courtiers to show pity.

The quartet in the final act of *Rigoletto* is possibly the most famous quartet in all opera. Hugo said of it, "If only I could make four characters in my plays speak at the same time, and have the audience grasp the words and sentiments, I would obtain the very same effect." The quartet opens with the tenor line *"Bella figlia dell'amore,"* against which the other three characters come in: Maddalena, the mezzo-soprano, with her chattering; the soprano, Gilda, with her breathless realization of betrayal; and the baritone, Rigoletto, insisting on vengeance from the bass line. The four parts are quite separate musically, but together they add up to a psychological completeness that is unique.

Soon after the quartet comes the storm, and more innovations from Verdi. Flute and piccolo describe lightning, with cellos and double bass as low, rumbling thunder while — to slow, chromatic wailings — the moaning wind is described by an offstage male chorus.

But it is in the great duets that the heart of the opera is to be found. The first duet sets a scene of sinister gloom, with Rigoletto and Sparafucile conversing in whispers against a melody played by clarinets and bassoons, with muted cello and double-bass solos playing against divided strings. The effect is claustrophobic, with an unforgettable ending as Sparafucile sinks to a low F.

There are no less than three duets for Rigoletto and Gilda. The first expresses the love, care, and comfort each provides for the other. This is followed by Gilda's love duet with the Duke, which, surprisingly, closely echoes the music expressed by father and daughter. The duet in the second act, where father and daughter discover each other's shame, starts with an oboe solo that sets a mood of tragic melancholy. This flows into Rigoletto's *"Piangi, fanciulla"* ("Cry, child"), and on to final resolution as Rigoletto vows to avenge the daughter he loves. In the final duet, Gilda sobs broken lines against the anguished cries of her father. We realize the change in Gilda as the orchestra plays fragments of *"Caro nome,"* for this is no longer a young girl in love with the sound of a name, but a woman who has made the ultimate sacrifice for the man she loves. Rigoletto's last outpouring of grief as he recalls the curse brings the opera full circle.

The story of *Rigoletto* is one of many dualities: of Verdi's own balance between the lyrical and dramatic elements of the plot; Gilda's growth from innocence to tragic heroine; of the Duke's ambivalence as to whether he is or is not truly in love; and, most of all, the character of Rigoletto. The stunted, ugly, vicious court jester is contrasted with the tenderness he expresses for his daughter. His emotional instability evokes pity and perhaps even empathy in audiences, for it is easy to understand the fluctuations and swings from one side of one's nature to the other. Rigoletto's situation is extreme, requiring extreme measures to reach resolution. Judgment, when it comes, is final, irrevocable, and heart-wrenching. Verdi has reached into the soul of this blighted man and transformed him in unforgettable music and song.

♪

Bibliography

Budden, Julian, *The Operas of Verdi*, Vol. 1, Oxford University Press, 1973.

Dramas of Victor Hugo, translated by F.L. Slous, President Publishing Co., New York [nd].

English National Opera Guide 15, *Rigoletto*, Nicholas John (Ed.), John Calder (Publishers), London, 1982.

A Marriage of Words and Music

Le Nozze di Figaro

Every object has two faces, and wedlock, bringing many graces, brings also troubles in a bevy.

Mozart to his sister, 18 August 1784

A white veil, a lady's ribbon, and a pin draw us into the roller-coaster action of *Le Nozze di Figaro* (The Marriage of Figaro). Based on the play by Caron de Beaumarchais, Mozart's work is radical and provocative. The overture, which contains none of the music in the opera, anticipates an evening of mischief and intrigue. Its central theme, a favorite topic of Mozart's, is the war of the sexes. The mercurial lightness of the overture dances its way into the opening scene, in which Figaro, valet to Count Almaviva, is discussing wedding plans with his fiancée, Susanna. What could be simpler?

It was said of Beaumarchais, the man who created Figaro, that he had but one character — Figaro, who was himself. A wit and an adventurer, Beaumarchais fought against injustice in the days prior to the French Revolution. He wrote a series of three plays: *Le Barbier de Séville* (1775), *La Folle Journée ou Le Mariage de Figaro* (1784), and *La Mère Coupable* (The Guilty Mother) (1797). *Le Mariage* was banned by Louis XVI, who saw social criticism in Beaumarchais's impertinent text. It was not until the intercession of his wife, Marie Antoinette, that permission was granted for its performance. Napoleon later described the play as "revolution in action."

Lorenzo da Ponte, the colorful librettist with whom Mozart collaborated on his three greatest operas — *Le Nozze di Figaro, Così fan Tutte,* and *Don Giovanni* — first met Mozart in Vienna, when the two men discussed the possibility of making Beaumarchais's *Figaro* into an opera. Since the Emperor, Joseph II, had banned all performances of the play, both knew that an opera based on it would run into censorship problems. As Poet to the Imperial Theatres, da Ponte went to Joseph and assured him, "I have written an opera, not a comedy, and I have left out anything which might offend the delicacy and decency of an entertainment at which your Majesty might preside. As to [Mozart's] music, it is remarkably beautiful." Joseph invited Mozart to play the music for him and, realizing that da Ponte was right, allowed the opera to go ahead.

Mozart's collaboration with da Ponte was one of magical proportions. In 1781 Mozart had written to his father, "In an opera the poetry must be altogether the obedient daughter of the music." Da Ponte was willing to be subordinate to Mozart's greater intellectual depth and understanding of the theatre. His own great contributions were good craftsmanship, wit, excellent plot construction, graceful verse, and insightful characterization.

The première was held in Vienna in 1786 and was successful; later the same year it played in Prague, where it caused a sensation. Mozart reported, "Here they talk of nothing but *Figaro*. Nothing is played, sung, or whistled but *Figaro*. No opera is drawing audiences like *Figaro*. Certainly a great honor for me" (January 1787). Brahms said of the opera, "Each number is a miracle."

Mozart communicates on many levels; *Figaro* is a true marriage of words and music, a Mozartian world in which a marriage of true love is also a marriage of true minds. He presents a musical language in which certain keys describe certain emotions: F-minor represents sadness and lament; A-major is the key of young love; G-minor hints at illicit sex. Puns and jokes are heard in the music; when, for instance, Figaro describes the horns on the heads of cuckolded men, the French horns echo his words.

Called an "Opera Buffa in Four Acts," *Figaro* is set during the course of one crazy day (*"La Folle Journée"*) near Seville. There are eleven characters, more than was usual for the Court Opera. The soprano Nancy Storace, of Italian/British birth, sang Susanna at the première. Due to difficulties with her top notes, Mozart scored all of Susanna's music low; so low that today the role is sometimes sung by mezzo-sopranos.

An Irish tenor, Michael Kelly (or, as he called himself in Europe, Michele Ochelli), doubled the roles of Basilio and the lawyer, Don Curzio. Kelly reported at the time, "Mozart was on stage in his crimson pelisse and gold-laced cocked hat, giving time to the orchestra. Benucci [Figaro] gave *"Non più andrai"* with the greatest animation and power of voice. Mozart, *sotto voce*, was repeating, "Bravo! Bravo! Benucci!" The musicians applauded, beating their bows against the music desks. "The little man acknowledged, by repeated bows, his thanks for the enthusiastic applause."

The stage manager, Bussani, doubled the roles of Dr. Bartolo and the gardener, Antonio, with a very fast costume change. His wife sang the first Cherubino with difficulty because she could not remember the part. The young page is scored for a soprano; even in the Beaumarchais play, Cherubino was to be played by a woman. Mozart smuggled a 12-year-old German girl into the theatre to sing the role of Barbarina. This young girl, five years later, sang the first Pamina.

It is interesting how the three plays of Beaumarchais have evolved over time: from his *Barber of Seville* (1775) to Paisiello's *Barber* in 1782, to Rossini's great *Barber of Seville* in 1816. Beaumarchais's *Le Mariage de Figaro* was immortalized in Mozart's opera in 1786. Richard Strauss's *Der Rosenkavalier* of 1911 resembles Mozart's *Figaro* in that both operas have young, cherubic cavaliers sung by women: Cherubino in *The Marriage of Figaro*, and Octavian, the Knight of the Silver Rose, in *Der Rosenkavalier*. Both operas set the tone in a bedroom: Mozart's Figaro is measuring his, while Strauss's opera starts with the Marschallin (the Countess) actually in bed with Octavian (Cherubino). Beaumarchais's third play, *La Mère Coupable*, became an opera by Darius Milhaud in 1966. The most contemporary treatment of Beaumarchais is John Corigliano's 1991 *Ghosts of Versailles*, which features Beaumarchais himself, Marie Antoinette, and the children of *La Mère Coupable*.

The opening-night audience at *The Marriage of Figaro* in Vienna in May 1786 would have known that Count Almaviva was a nobleman of Seville, and the highest judge in Andalusia. About to be sent as ambassador for Spain to England, he is a man of some clout. In *The Barber of Seville*, Almaviva, bored with life in Madrid, goes to Seville to pursue a young woman with whom he has fallen in love. The young woman, Rosina, is a ward of Dr. Bartolo, who has his own plans to marry her. With the help of Figaro, the general factotum, and the mischievous Rosina, Bartolo is outwitted and the Count and Rosina escape, marry, and, one presumes, walk off into the sunset.

That is, until *The Marriage of Figaro*, which is set some three years later. The Count, bored now with married life, seeks diversion, and thinks he has found it on his doorstep with Susanna, his wife's maidservant. His wife, Rosina, the Countess, is not entirely comfortable in her new role as a lady. Her friend, the barber Figaro, promoted to the Count's valet, plans marriage to Susanna. Dr. Bartolo is retained in the Count's household, as is Marcellina, the onetime governess of Rosina who is now housekeeper to the Count. Basilio, the scurrilous music teacher from *The Barber of Seville*, still provides music and, more important, acts as liaison between the unfaithful Count and the women he desires.

The opera begins with a domestic scene as Susanna explains to the somewhat slow Figaro that the proximity of their room to the Count's means that the Count plans to "Bribe me to grant him his feudal right as lord and master on the night of our wedding." *Le droit du Seigneur* was a feudal custom whereby the Lord had the right to have sex with his vassal's bride-to-be on the eve of the wedding. This medieval tradition was never actually law, but it was an ugly practice that servants were powerless to prevent. In reality, the custom was brought to an end long before *Figaro*. It was Beaumarchais who had the Count rescind his right saying, "The abolition of a shameful custom is no more than an acknowledgment of what is due to common decency." Now he is having second thoughts, for he plans to possess Susanna before the wedding night. To this end he has promised the couple a dowry and a bedroom close to his. Susanna, however, has a mind of her own, and will not comply. The Count is constantly frustrated as she persists in denying him her favors; in this, Almaviva and Don Giovanni are related, for neither man succeeds in his pursuit of women in the course of either opera.

Almaviva, an aristocrat who is used to getting his way without question, is confused and frustrated at every turn: Susanna will not have him, Figaro is impertinent, and the young page, Cherubino, seems to be underfoot every time he approaches a woman. In the double standard of the time it was acceptable for the Count to be unfaithful, but the same did not hold true for his wife. When Almaviva hears that Rosina is possibly having an affair, he is furious, jealous, his honor at stake. Almaviva is manipulated by all the major characters in the plot, outwitted at every turn by his servants and even by his wife. Unaware of the extent to which he is made to look a fool, he continues blindly in the old ways, unforgiving and stubborn. The Count's sole aria, at the beginning of the third act, comes when it seems Susanna will not succumb and he rages against what he perceives to be the injustice of it all, *"Vedro mentr'io sospiro"*:

> *Must I see a serf of mine happy, while I am left to sigh?*
> *Must I see her who roused in me a passion*
> *United by the hand of love to a slave?*
> *You were not born, bold fellow, [Figaro] to cause me torment*
> *And laugh at my discomfort.*

The Countess, Rosina, appears alone in her rooms at the start of the second act. She sings of the loss of her husband's love in a cavatina, *"Porgi, amor,"* "Give me back my loved one or, in mercy, let me die." Isolated by her marriage and abandoned by her husband, Rosina is no longer the vital, mischievous young woman of *The Barber of Seville*. She is distanced and set apart, confiding only in her maid, Susanna, and Figaro. Yet a sense of fun has not entirely left Rosina, for she welcomes the attentions of Cherubino, the young page, who loves her, wears her ribbon, and composes love songs to her. When cornered in a compromising situation (she and Susanna are dressing Cherubino as a woman), the Countess stands her ground as her husband unexpectedly knocks at the door and demands to be let in.

Ignoring the social conventions that made them mistress and servant, Rosina and Susanna are like sisters. The two women refuse to become rivals sexually jealous of one another because of the Count's behavior. They are good friends and loyal, an unusual occurrence for two women in opera. The strength of their alliance gives the opera a poignancy that is rare. In 1786, these two women, mistress and maid, stood together united against the tyranny of the Count and the ways of the *ancien régime*.

Rosina can be portrayed either as an abandoned woman or as a woman who fights for what she believes in, for it is she, not Figaro, who devises the plan to bring the Count to his knees begging forgiveness. She dictates a letter to Susanna suggesting the Count meet Susanna in the garden later that night, only the woman he will meet will not be Susanna but the Countess herself dressed in her maid's clothes. In a lovely duet, the Countess dictates, "How sweet the breeze will be this evening in the pine-grove." "The pine-grove?" Susanna queries. "He'll understand," Rosina assures her. In lieu of a seal, the two women affix the note with a pin from the Countess's lapel.

The Countess hesitates momentarily at the audacity of her plan; she is taking a risk, and she is not comfortable, "To what humiliation am I reduced by a cruel husband who, after loving me, then neglected and deceived me, in a strange mixture of infidelity, jealousy, and disdain, now forces me to seek help from my servants?" She reminisces, in one of opera's loveliest arias, *"Dove sono,"* "Where are those happy moments of sweetness and pleasure? If only my constancy in loving him always could bring hope of changing his ungrateful heart." But she goes through with the plan and, in the end, when the Count is made to realize, before his entire assembled staff, that the woman he was making love to in the arbor was not Susanna but his wife, he is at last contrite and begs forgiveness. The final measures of the opera are Rosina's moments of sheer transcendence as she forgives her errant husband.

Figaro is the figurehead who makes this opera revolutionary; he is the servant who, along with Susanna, the Countess, and Cherubino, challenges the system on behalf of servants, women, and the young. All three triumph over the dissolute Count.

Figaro is the same jaunty character we met in *The Barber of Seville,* but in *The Marriage of Figaro* his plans come to naught; everything backfires. He attempts to have the Count perform a little ceremony of placing the symbol of purity, a crown of orange blossoms and its white veil, on Susanna's head, but his master keeps putting him off. He sends the Count an anonymous note stating that the Countess has an assignation that night with a lover, but that misfires. At the start, he has no idea that the Count has designs on his Susanna until she tells him and, at the end, he has no idea of who is meeting whom in the arbors in the garden.

Yet Figaro, sung by the beloved bass Benucci at the première, sings three of the opera's great arias. In the first he addresses the Count mockingly as "little Count," (*"Se vuol ballare, Signor Contino,"*): "If, my dear Count, you feel like dancing, it's I who'll call the tune." Figaro expresses his determination in this little cavatina set to an aristocratic minuet. He ends the first act with a lively march, *"Non più andrai,"* painting a painful picture of war to Cherubino, who has been flirting with Susanna and who has just been banished to the army: "No more, you amorous butterfly, will you go fluttering round night and day."

In the last act, Figaro mistakenly believes that Susanna has indeed agreed to meet the Count, and he vents his anger and frustration in an extraordinary musical portrait of jealousy in

"Aprite un po'quegl' occhi,": "Open your eyes, you rash and foolish men, and look at these women, and see them as they are." This is another instance of the double standard that prevailed in which women were seen as fickle, while men could act exactly as they chose. Even Basilio reiterates this fact when he sings, *"Così fan tutte le belle!"* "All women act like that." This line, *"Così fan tutte,"* went on to become the title of Mozart and da Ponte's next opera, with the self-same melody appearing in *Così*'s overture.

Susanna, arguably the central character, is the only truly virtuous person in the opera. Living by her wits, she manages to sidestep the Count's advances by telling both Figaro and the Countess about his advances. She loves Figaro and will be married to him. She is faithful to her mistress, the Countess, as both her confidante and partner in planning the exposure of the Count's indiscretions. Susanna is filled with a *joie de vivre* that Mozart so tellingly brings to life in her music. On stage for most of the opera, she interacts with the other characters in duets and ensembles. Her aria in the last act is one of the great testimonies to love when she sings, accompanied by strings, flute, oboe, and bassoon, *"Deh vieni, non tardar,"* ("Do not delay, oh bliss, come where love calls thee to joy"). The mood is one of ecstatic tranquility and harmony. For the singer, however, this aria, coming near the end of four long acts, is a major test; the voice will certainly be warmed up, but the singer may be exhausted.

Cherubino, a new member of the cast of since *The Barber*, is a page to the Count. He calls the Countess his godmother for, as was the custom of the time, young men from good families often became pages (or, in 20th-century terminology, interns), to serve in a nobleman's house in order to be educated in manners. Cherubino is receiving an education that is probably not the one his parents had in mind, for Cherubino is in love with love. He is caught by the Count flirting with Barbarina, the gardener's daughter. He flirts with Susanna in her room and has to hide quickly when the Count appears unexpectedly. Discovery nearly happens a third time when Cherubino is in the Countess' rooms declaring his love for her by way of a song, *"Voi che sapete."* In this arietta Cherubino describes his nascent feelings of love: "I have a feeling, full of desire, which now is pleasure, now torment. My spirit all ablaze, next moment I turn to ice." The Countess is sympathetic to his yearning but, in *The Marriage of Figaro*, does not encourage the boy. Cherubino is devastated when the Count assigns him a commission in the army and orders him to leave at once.

His very name a diminutive of the angelic cherubs of love, Cherubino disturbs the hearts and dreams of the women in the opera. Fluttering and winged, even Figaro refers to him as *"farfallone amoroso,"* ("amorous butterfly"). Kierkegaard, in his book, *Either/Or*, describes Cherubino in his three stages of love: the first stage suggested by the page in *Figaro,* the second by the simple, seeking Papageno in *The Magic Flute*, and the third by the libertine Don Giovanni. Kierkegaard says of Cherubino, "The sensuous awakens to a hushed tranquillity; not to joy and gladness, but to a deep melancholy. Desire is not yet awake, but only a gloomy foreboding." Cherubino's first intimations of love are described in Mozart's music as "quiet desire, quiet longing, and quiet ecstasy. Desire, in Cherubino, is only a presentiment for he only dreams of love."

The third couple in the opera are Marcellina and Bartolo, an unlikely pair. Marcellina appears near the start of the opera angrily complaining to Dr. Bartolo that she has rights. In her hand is a contract, a contract with Figaro, who had borrowed a sizeable sum of money from her and who, the contract states, must marry her if he does not repay the money. With Figaro's marriage to Susanna imminent, Marcellina is determined to see justice done and marry Figaro herself. Bartolo eagerly agrees to help her since he has his own axe to grind with Figaro, who was responsible for the Count's elopement and marriage to Rosina, the ward Bartolo planned to marry in *The Barber of Seville*. Marcellina's angry denouncement of Figaro fits nicely into the Count's plans. If Susanna agrees to his proposals, the Count will give her and Figaro a dowry that would pay off the debt to Marcellina. But if Susanna will not acquiesce, the Count will stop the marriage by withholding the dowry. As the Count gets increasingly angry at Susanna's refusals, he calls together a farcical court of law with Marcellina, Figaro, Don Curzio, a stuttering lawyer, and himself as judge.

Marcellina states her case. Don Curzio gives his opinion: "Pay up or marry her!" The Count is delighted. Figaro says he cannot marry without his parents' permission, for he is of noble birth. His parents, he says, abandoned him at birth, leaving only a birthmark on his arm as identification. Marcellina gasps as she recognizes the birthmark of the son she bore Dr. Bartolo. The infant had been stolen and had the same mark. "Raffaello!" she cries out. There follows one of the funniest scenes in opera, as the truth dawns that Figaro is indeed the son of Marcellina and Bartolo. Figaro is amazed — and relieved, for now he cannot marry Marcellina, his mother. Marcellina is ecstatic, Bartolo stunned, Don Curzio annoyed, and the Count furious at this new frustration. Susanna comes in at this moment, astonished to find Figaro in Marcellina's arms. The whole recognition scene is played again for her benefit. Bartolo, though not entirely happy at the ways things are working out, does the honorable thing and agrees to marry Marcellina; there will be a double wedding. The F-major sextet that happens at this point is thrilling, expressing simultaneously the differing thoughts and emotions of the six characters.

The "pay-up or marry" ruling may seem strange to us today, but there was precedent for it very close to home. When Mozart was a penniless musician, he stayed with the Weber family, a mother and four daughters. He spent so much time with Constanze that people began to talk — was Mozart going to marry her or not?

If not, then Constanze was being compromised. The mother, eager to see her daughters wed, came up with a solution by asking Mozart to sign a document that said if he did not marry Constanze he would pay the family a large sum of money. When she heard of this Constanze tore up the document, and Mozart married her anyway.

The remaining characters, according to the operatic tradition of the time, each had to have at least one aria. Dr. Bartolo's aria comes in the first act, when he sings *"La vendetta,"* a tirade against Figaro, on whom he wants revenge. The arias of Marcellina and Basilio, the music master, occur in the last act, and both are usually cut, which is a pity. Marcellina's aria is a rebuttal to Figaro's criticism of women. She sings, "We, poor women, who so love these men, are treated by the traitors with constant perfidy." Marcellina has a major change of heart when she finds she is Figaro's mother, and when she learns that Bartolo will marry her after all. Now she takes Susanna's part and assures Figaro that Susanna can be trusted.

Basilio's aria is an odd little treatise that says it is dangerous to clash with "important people" because the lesser man cannot win. "Fate made me realize that shame, dangers, humiliation, and death can be avoided beneath an ass's skin" (i.e., if I stay in my place as a servant). After all that has gone before with Figaro and Susanna constantly challenging and outwitting the Count, Basilio's words are surprising.

The story of *The Marriage of Figaro* is complex, but accessible in performance. Moving away from the traditional long string of arias, Mozart has his characters interact with one another in duets and ensembles. The ensembles that end Acts II (a twenty-minute finale of three movements), and IV (sung by all eleven principals) are thrilling and exciting.

Humor was a great strength of Mozart's. In *Figaro* there are many *coups de théâtre,* or great surprises, that provoke laughter at the human foibles of characters in whom we all too often see ourselves. The hide-and-seek nonsense of the first act is broad comedy: Cherubino hides in Susanna's room as the Count enters, the Count hides (almost in the same place) as Basilio enters, and Cherubino finally is discovered. The closet scene is amusing when the audience is let in on the secret as to who is and who is not hiding in the closet. The recognition scene, in which Figaro finds out that Marcellina is his mother, is hilarious; this time the audience is as surprised as the characters on stage. There is more: the dressing-up of Cherubino, the drunken gardener and his broken flower pots, the stuttering lawyer. The final *coup de théâtre* is pure chaos, as everyone is confused as to who is meeting whom in which arbor in the garden.

But finally it all unravels and truth is revealed: the Count is caught making love to his own wife, believing her to be Susanna. This is the transcendent moment when the Countess forgives her contrite husband. Her absolution ends all the misunderstandings in the shadowed garden; it is a blessing in music. Rosina rises above personal pain and grief, forgiving herself, and Figaro, whose intrigues and brief doubt of Susanna's faithfulness are forgiven; Cherubino, for his dalliances in his first hesitant steps on the path to love; and Marcellina and Bartolo, whose petty jealousies nearly destroyed the happiness of the onetime barber and his bride. Only Susanna comes through the crazy day with her spirit (and body) intact, eager for her wedding to Figaro, whom she truly loves. The Count, we sense, will sin again, but for this perfect moment, the forgiveness of the Countess, and Mozart, are enough.

♪

Bibliography

Beaumarchais, Caron de, *The Barber of Seville* and *The Marriage of Figaro*, John Wood (Transl.), New York, 1978.

Brophy, Brigid, *Mozart the Dramatist*, Harcourt, Brace & World Inc., New York, 1964.

Conrad, Peter, *A Song of Love and Death*, Poseidon Press, New York, 1987.

FitzLyon, April, *Lorenzo da Ponte, A Biography*, Riverrun Press, New York, 1982.

Goldovsky, Boris, *The Adult Mozart: A Personal Perspective*, Vol. 1, 1991.

Kierkegaard, Søren, *Either/Or*, Princeton University Press, 1959.

Letters of Mozart, Hans Mersmann (Ed.), Dorset Press, New York, 1986.

Newman, Ernest, *Great Operas*, Vol. 1, Vintage Books, New York, 1959.

Osborne, Charles, *The Complete Operas of Mozart*, Da Capo Press, New York 1978.

Osborne, Charles, *The Complete Operas of Verdi*, A.A. Knopf, New York, 1969.

Phillips-Matz, Mary Jane, *Verdi, A Biography*, Oxford University Press, 1993.

Music Becomes Elektra

Elektra

Do I hear the music? The music comes from me! — Elektra

Steeped in blood, the depraved Klytemnestra and her lover kill her husband, Agamemnon, in his bath with an axe. Klytemnestra's daughter, Elektra, dreams of bloody vengeance, while her son, Orestes, follows his destiny in murdering his mother to avenge his father. Klytemnestra indiscriminately sacrifices one animal after another in a desperate attempt to appease the Gods. Orestes, her son, will bring peace, the peace of death, as he coldly calculates and plans his mother's murder, while his sister Elektra dances madly in the palace courtyard, where the flagstones run with blood.

This is Greek tragedy at its most violent, brought to life in the music of post-romantic expressionism. This is Richard Strauss at his most extreme and, many would argue, his most magnificent. The stabbing vocal lines and vast orchestral canvas of this relatively short work are awesome and horrifying. In his book, *Recollections and Reflections,* Strauss said, "In [*Elektra*] I penetrated the uttermost limits of harmony, psychological polyphony, and the receptivity of modern ears." He graphically evokes the horrors of the tragedy's harsh scenes — the outcast Elektra forced to eat with the dogs, the brutal whipping of a servant who speaks up for her, the frightening leading of animals to sacrifice. The internal forces that drive this desperate family are probed in the music: the blood lust of Klytemnestra, the primitive madness of Elektra, the icy resolve of Orestes. Elektra's sister, Chrysothemis, who longs to escape the destiny of her royal blood, seems unnatural in her desire to be normal. Hate, depravity, and revenge rule this cursed family. The lust for blood passes directly from mother to daughter, Klytemnestra to Elektra, and from father to son, Agamemnon to Orestes. No wonder people asked in 1909 whether Strauss had gone too far. They thought they had heard and seen it all in *Salome*, the biblical story of Herod's dysfunctional family. Strauss used Oscar Wilde's sensational play as the source of that opera, but with *Elektra*, he turned to a new translation of Sophocles play, *Electra,* by the poet and scholar Hugo von Hofmannsthal, the librettist with whom Strauss would collaborate on six of his greatest operas.

Hofmannsthal was a Viennese who earned his doctorate at Vienna University with a study on the development of Victor

Hugo, but poetry and verse drama attracted him most. In 1903 he wrote his own version of the story of *Electra* from the ancient Greek myth of Agamemnon, the great king who led the Greeks into battle in the Trojan War. In the 5th century B.C. three plays were written on the Agamemnon/Electra myth: by Aeschylus in his trilogy, the *Oresteia;* by Sophocles in *Electra;* and by Euripides in *Orestes.* Hofmannsthal chose the Sophocles version.

Living in early 20th-century Vienna at the time of Freud's research into psychoanalysis, Hofmannsthal was interested in the psychological motivation behind the characters. He left behind Sophocles' arguments about the Trojan War, the intervention of the Gods, oracles, prophetic visions, and royal dynasties, in favor of issues of myth, hysteria, fear, dreams, psychosexual fantasies, terrifying nightmares, and psychic trauma. Agamemnon, Elektra's murdered father, strides across the action of the play, unseen but ever present, bearing out Wagner's belief that art and music can make the unconscious conscious. Hofmannsthal said of Sophocles' play, "I have not touched the figures. I have only rearranged the cloak of words which hung around their bronze existences, so that advocacy is put into the shade, and poetry is brought into the light." When the opera was produced in 1909 in Dresden, it met with mixed reviews. To negative critics, Strauss responded, "When a mother is slain on the stage, do they expect me to write a violin concerto?"

Every version of Elektra's story unleashes a storm of wild, primitive behavior in its protagonist, yet Strauss, a seemingly conservative man, maintained control of this challenging subject. At this time in his career, he was famous both as a conductor and composer of tone poems, works that told stories in music: *Till Eulenspiegel's Merry Pranks, Don Juan, Don Quixote, Also sprach Zarathustra.* With opera, he took the tone poem one step further. By adding voices to the orchestra, he could paint with a whole new palette. He said, "My vocal style has the pace of a stage play and frequently comes into conflict with the figuring and polyphony of the orchestra, so that none but the best conductors can establish the balance of volume and speed between singer and baton. The struggle between word and music has been the problem of my life right from the beginning." He and the conductor of the première, Ernst von Schuch, disagreed when the orchestra played quietly so Klytemnestra could be heard. Strauss was not happy. He complained to the conductor, "Louder! Louder! I can still hear Frau Schumann-Heink."

Strauss required enormous orchestras; over one hundred instruments are scored for *Elektra*. He loved the high, clear sound of the soprano voice and reflected it in his music. Like Wagner, his mentor, Strauss wrote for large orchestras and made superhuman demands of his singers. Most of *Elektra* is scored for women's voices: the contralto Klytemnestra and her two soprano daughters, Elektra and Chrysothemis. Though the men in the opera, Orestes and Aegisthus, appear late, their roles are important; Orestes is a major protagonist, and Aegisthus plays a vital cameo role.

The Greek story of the cursed House of Atreus tells of the great king Agamemnon, who, though victorious in the Trojan War, had sacrificed his daughter, Iphigenia, so that the Gods would grant him a favorable wind to sail to war. Klytemnestra, his wife, was present at the slaughter of their daughter, and, in revenge, took as a lover Agamemnon's enemy, Aegisthus. Upon Agamemnon's victorious return, Klytemnestra and Aegisthus murdered him in his bath. Klytemnestra believes the act was justified — she has avenged her daughter's death, and Aegisthus has avenged the wrongs to his family. Blood for blood. Following the murder, Agamemnon and Klytemnestra's young son, Orestes, is sent away secretly to be raised in safety. Elektra, filled with blind hatred toward her mother and Aegisthus, is treated like an animal at court. She lives only for revenge. Orestes grows to manhood and, on learning the truth of his noble birth and the murder of his father, returns, as an act of honor, to kill Klytemnestra and Aegisthus. Elektra assists him in the murder.

Strauss's opera is composed in one long, gripping act. There is little release from the tension, which builds from the first electrifying chords in the brass. Strauss called the work a Tragedy in One Act, not an opera. The scene is set in the inner courtyard of the royal palace at Mycenae; the two huge doors of the palace can be seen at the back of the stage. It is evening; light comes from the wavering flames of torches in the walls. There is no overture, only the harsh motif of the slain king — the majestic, fortissimo chords of the dead father, Agamemnon. The chords permeate the action, clear and direct at the start, then becoming embroiled in ugly harmonies and gradually disintegrating at the lowest end as the action progresses. Elektra, obsessed by her father's memory, hears them everywhere; her father seems to cry out for vengeance through her. The chords are chopped off, attacked, slaughtered in music, even as Agamemnon was slaughtered. The murdered chords are heard again and again at key moments in the opera, a relentless reminder of the restless soul of the dead king.

Strauss explicitly describes the meaning of words in his music. As the curtain opens, a number of serving maids talk spitefully about Elektra, for this is "the hour when she howls for her father." They call her a beast and a wild cat, "forever crouching over the smell of carrion." The orchestra hisses and scratches as the maids talk of the cat-like Elektra. Fear fills the palace under the despotic rule of Klytemnestra and Aegisthus. A maid who speaks up for Elektra ("I want to throw myself down before her and kiss her feet. Is she not a king's daughter?") is dragged offstage and beaten to the sound of lashing from the orchestra. These interpretive sections are not true motifs but are used by Strauss as effects. In the short opening section the maids give background details of the plot, and the tension builds as they sing of the bestial Elektra.

Elektra now appears, disheveled and dirty, a wildness in her eyes. In Hofmannsthal's notes for the play, he describes Elektra's entrance as "alone with spots of red light falling diagonally out of the branches of the fig-tree onto the ground and onto the walls like blood-stains." *Elektra* is lit by torches, a flickering half-light evocative of dreams. Elektra's first words: "Alone, alas, all alone. Father has gone to his cold grave," begin her long, lonely lament, a mantra sung every evening to keep vividly alive the traumatic memories of years before. Elektra calls her father's name (again the Agamemnon chord, but this time the octaves are empty with dissonances; the King is dead) and relives the horror of his death: the bath in which he was slain, Aegisthus dragging him across the palace floors bathed in blood, Klytemnestra's death blows with the axe — the axe Elektra has hidden, and with which her father's murder will be avenged. She rails against the horror of her mother's action and the equally appalling horror of her mother's consorting with the killer, Aegisthus. Elektra begs her father, "show yourself to your child as you did yesterday, like a shadow in the recess of the wall." The strings describe her physical, child-like yearning in a beautifully soft, romantic melody. Her mood suddenly shifts. Blood must flow; the strings describe a wave of blood, "As all time pours down from the stars, so the blood from a hundred throats will pour onto your grave. Horses and hounds will be slaughtered" (this to serious echoes of *The Ride of the Valkyries*), and then, "We, your flesh and blood, your son Orestes, and your daughters, we three, when all this has been performed, will dance around your grave." The music, at the end of the long monologue, turns into a macabre waltz as Elektra envisions the dance that is to come.

Lost in this dream and caught up in her aria, Elektra is not aware of the approach of her sister, Chrysothemis. She turns on her, "What do you want, daughter of Klytemnestra?" Chrysothemis tells Elektra that she overheard their mother and Aegisthus planning to lock Elektra away in a dark tower. Elektra merely laughs in broken rhythms while Chrysothemis, tonal and romantic, begs Elektra to end her hate. "If it were not for you, they would let us go." Chrysothemis is terrified, and wants to leave, to live, to have children "before my body shrivels up." She is frightened and alone. She and Elektra "sit forever like birds hung up on a pole, and no one comes, no brother, no one." In a long and lovely solo, Chrysothemis breaks down and weeps. Her words fall on deaf ears; Elektra hears nothing. A disturbing, dissonant procession sounds in the distance. Chrysothemis tells Elektra that Klytemnestra, their mother, is on her way in a foul mood, for she has had a nightmare about Orestes and murder in the palace. Chrysothemis leaves; Elektra faces her mother alone.

The meeting of Klytemnestra and Elektra is the heart of the opera. In Strauss's words, the agonizing march is "A straining and dragging of beasts; muffled scoldings; a quickly stifled outcry; the sound of a whiplash; animals struggling to stand up; a staggering onward." This is tragedy, a goat song. (The word "tragedy" in Greek means "goat-song," a song chanted as goats were sacrificed to honor Dionysus.) In the midst of this goat song, Klytemnestra makes her appearance, her body gross, her face bloated and sallow, the lids of her eyes heavy. She is covered with gems and talismans, amulets to ward off evil. She leans on her servants, the Confidante and the Trainbearer.

At the end of the shattering crescendo that accompanies her entrance, Klytemnestra points her staff at Elektra. "See how she rears up with her neck swelling and hisses at me!" Klytemnestra blames the gods. Elektra reproaches her, "But you yourself are a goddess?" Klytemnestra, believing her daughter to be in a receptive mood, comes down to speak with her, sending away her servants. She describes the nightmares that paralyze her strength with visions of appalling creatures crawling over her, and asks if Elektra knows a cure. Elektra (Hofmannsthal?), somehow aware of

Freud's statement that "a dream is a disguised fulfilment of a suppressed wish," tells Klytemnestra that she knows the cure: she knows the sacrifice required by the gods. Elektra plays with her mother. Klytemnestra asks what she must do. "When the appointed victim bleeds beneath the axe, then you will dream no more," Elektra assures her. The victim will be a woman, a wife. The killing will be any time, any place. A man will deal the blow, "a stranger from our house." Then, abruptly, Elektra appears to change the subject. "Will you not let my brother come home?" Klytemnestra angrily warns Elektra that if she does not reveal the sacrificial rites, "Blood will flow so I may sleep again." Elektra drops the pretense and graphically spells out the horrors her mother will endure, for she is to be the victim and Orestes the killer. He will seek her out and pursue her through the palace, as in a hunt, until the axe falls: "Then you will dream no more." The orchestra describes the baying of hounds as they run their prey to earth. Elektra shrieks wildly at her mother, who is frozen with horror. The tension breaks as the Confidante runs in and whispers in Klytemnestra's ear. Her expression changes to one of triumph as she calls for lights and returns exultant to the palace. Elektra is left wondering why her mother is so pleased.

Chrysothemis returns with the answer: a messenger has brought news that Orestes is dead! Elektra denies it, "It is not true!" A young servant, the first male to be heard in the opera, runs in demanding a horse to bring the news of Orestes' death to Aegisthus (the orchestra gallops alongside). Elektra absorbs the news and comes to a decision — she and Chrysothemis must do the deed together. Chrysothemis is appalled. Elektra breaks into a waltz and promises to serve her sister like a slave if she will agree to be a partner in their mother's murder. Elektra praises her sister's physical beauty and strength. She promises to bathe her for the bridegroom who will come after the deed is done. She will tend Chrysothemis' child. She says, "I will creep around you, sink my roots into you, and infuse my will into your blood." Chrysothemis backs away in terror and flees as Elektra curses her: *"Sei verflucht!"*

Elektra falls to her knees as, alone by the wall, accompanied only by digging strings, she digs for the axe that killed her father. She does not notice the arrival of a stranger in the courtyard. Elektra is startled. "Who are you, What do you want?" He tells her he has come to visit the Queen to bring news of Orestes' death. Elektra wails at the news. Servants run out from the house and, recognizing Orestes, kiss his garment. Orestes is horrified at his sister's appearance, but Elektra is ecstatic at the return of her brother, the moment she has dreamed of for so long. This is a classic Greek Recognition scene: Elektra's recognition of her brother (as much an inner recognition of herself) turns her despair to triumph. Violins and violas express her joy, her relief, her compassion. This is one of the most beautiful and moving parts of the opera. Orestes assures his sister that he has come to take revenge, but he trembles at the deed he must do. To kill Aegisthus is to obey the ancient code of honor, but matricide is something for which he will be pursued by the Furies. Elektra encourages him with a strange litany of praise: "Happy is the man who does the deed, happy the man who digs the axe out of the ground, happy the man who holds the torch for him."

In spite of the high-decibel rush of emotion that accompanies this reunion, no sound comes from the palace until Orestes' old guardian appears and tells him, "The Queen is waiting inside; the maids search for you." Orestes enters the house; Elektra is left alone. The basses growl, explosive outbursts come from the orchestra as Elektra waits. She remembers too late that she forgot to give Orestes the axe. Then, a scream from Klytemnestra. Elektra leaps to her feet: "Strike again," she cries out. The maids run back and forth in confusion as Aegisthus arrives at the palace gates demanding "Lights!" Elektra takes a torch off the wall and offers to light his way. She tells him strangers are in the palace "making merry with the Queen." Aegisthus passes through the doors and moments later his death cries are heard. "Does no one hear me?" he calls out. Elektra replies violently, "Agamemnon hears you" as the great chords thunder out from the orchestra.

Now comes the final terrible dance. Elektra, triumphant, is increasingly unaware of her surroundings. "The thousands who carry torches are waiting for me; I must lead the dance." Chrysothemis comes to her sister, jubilant that her brother has killed their mother, but Elektra is exhausted and can barely respond. Lost in her own world, she summons up her final shreds of strength to dance a ritual dance rooted in earth, a dance without a name, to the rhythm of a dark waltz. Chrysothemis calls to her sister. "Dance on," Elektra sings, oblivious to all but her own sense of exultation and completion. Now, at last, she is free. Elektra falls dead as Chrysothemis runs to the closed doors of the palace crying out her brother's name, "Orestes! Orestes!" The Agamemnon chord blasts forth one last time, and the opera ends on a full C-major chord that brings vindication and rest to the tortured soul of Agamemnon and to his daughter as the drama ends.

In *Elektra* the music is the protagonist, the main player, the voice, the heart and soul of the work. The tension in the orchestra builds from start to finish in what is sometimes called the "crescendo effect," in which one climax comes hurtling on the heels of another until it is all over. The music takes over when, in the long crescendo at the end, Elektra moves beyond words in her waltz of death. She asks the question, "Do I hear music? The music comes from me." Utterly absorbed in the sounds of the world she has created for herself, she *becomes* the music. The music emanates from the distressed woman who, in this one telling line, becomes the voice of the composer, Strauss. Liberation for Elektra is found not in words, but in music, in dance.

The drama in the opera is structured by Hofmannsthal in a symmetrical manner in seven distinct sections, sometimes called a "closed structure."

1 The Maids (Prologue)
2 Elektra's monologue
3 Elektra and Chrysothemis
4 Elektra and Klytemnestra
5 Elektra and Chrysothemis
6 Elektra and Orestes
7 The murders, Elektra's dance and death

The structure of the work provides dramatic cohesion, for the tension that builds in this family effectively cuts them off from the outside world; they are an enclosed unit. Musically, the symmetry of the sections is not unlike sonata-form structure. The center of the work is the Elektra/Klytemnestra scene, around which the two Elektra/Chrysothemis scenes are balanced. Elektra's monologue and her final scene and death balance each other, surrounding the mother/daughter center of the work. The Prologue (Greek chorus) stands alone, as does the great recognition scene between Elektra and Orestes. That the closed structure of the drama coexisted with the through-composed structure of the music was unique. Strauss and Hofmannsthal created a new form with the composition of *Elektra*.

In the end, one must ask: Why does tragedy, with its images of horror and suffering, bring us pleasure and satisfaction? What is the appeal of Greek drama? What is it that allows us to sit through the trauma of this story and emerge intact — or, more than that, satisfied with a sense of well being, of being cleansed, the evil washed away (albeit in a sea of blood!)? Aristotle, long ago, said the arts give pleasure because they satisfy basic needs of harmony and rhythm — musical terms. In tragedy there is satisfaction in recognizing and knowing, at some mysterious level, the trauma, horror, or joys that are common to all mankind. Harmony and rhythm in drama, and especially in music, please us, while exposure to terror and fear touches the dark edges of our human experience. Writers of great tragedy frighten us, then soften us with pity, thus purging our emotions as we recognize and grasp universal truths. Aristotle, in the fourth century B.C., called it "catharsis," a cleansing of the body and spirit. We work through feelings of both fear and pity in *Elektra* and recognize, in the end, something mysterious and universal in the tragedy of this ill-fated family.

George Bernard Shaw described it well when he talked of *Elektra*'s "atmosphere of malignant evil. The power with which it is done is not the power of the evil itself, but of the passion that detests and must and finally can destroy that evil, that is what makes the work great, and makes us rejoice in its horror."

♪

BIBLIOGRAPHY

Bokina, John, *Opera and Politics*, Yale University Press, 1997.

Cambridge Opera Handbooks: *Richard Strauss: Elektra*, Derrick Puffett (Ed.), Cambridge University Press, 1989.

Fergusson, Francis, *Aristotle's Poetics*, Hill and Wang, New York, 1961.

Mann, William, *A Critical Study of the Operas*, Cassell, London, 1964.

Osborne, Charles, *The Complete Operas of Richard Strauss*, Da Capo Press, New York, 1988.

Strauss, Richard, *Recollections and Reflections*, Willi Schuh (Ed.), Boosey and Hawkes, London, 1953.

A Greek Tragedy

Ermione

Gioacchino Rossini was already well established and jet-setting (in a carriage) around Europe, composing operas as fast as he could, when *Ermione* saw the light of day in 1819 at the Teatro San Carlo in Naples. He had composed three operas in 1818, one of them *Moses in Egypt*, an *opera seria* that is returning to the operatic repertoire today; and four operas in 1819, in Naples, Venice, and Milan. Rossini's productivity is almost unbelievable. His work expresses a verve, a lightness and freshness that are exhilarating. His music is kaleidoscopic, filled with contrasts. While often re-using earlier music, he argued that this was necessary in order to meet opera-house deadlines.

The life of a composer in the early 1800s was rigorous. Opera houses rarely presented the same operas over and over, as we do today. Italian audiences expected new operas from their composers every year. *Opera buffa* was the main fare of these audiences; they said of *opera seria* that tragedy and sadness gave them indigestion. Rossini, writing a happy ending to *Tancredi* to accommodate this sentiment, later wrote the true tragic ending, but audiences refused to accept it, and he had to revert to the first version. Berlioz said of Italian audiences of his day, "Music for the Italians is a sensual pleasure and nothing more. They want a score that, like a plate of macaroni, can be assimilated immediately without their having to think about it."

Jet-setting in those days was done with a horse and carriage. Vast distances over rough, often impassable roads made traveling a challenge. Rossini would set up a desk top in the carriage and compose as he moved from city to city. Composition for him was a job that required all his energy, for his parents and other relatives depended on him for support. Once composition was complete (often during rehearsals), Rossini would work with the singers, rewrite as needed, and, by contractual agreement, conduct the first three performances from the cembalo, or harpsichord. Once famous, he was constantly on the road, staging, conducting, and composing in an endless cycle. It is little wonder he chose to give it all up at the age of thirty-seven.

The strict formula for *opera buffa* and *seria* prescribed the form and number for set-pieces and ensembles; there was little use of chorus. One odd little aria, called an *aria del sorbetto*, was sung literally while the audience took refreshments (sorbet!) and gossiped. (One such aria was, ironically, considered the best music in one of Rossini's early operas.) These were formula operas using a form of libretto set down by Metastasio; formulas that went back to Gluck, and which were continued by Cimaroso, Cherubini, and Paisiello, the great composers of the earlier century. Opera had become static, almost a parody of itself.

In addition to the formulaic style, Rossini had to deal with contentious singers. Prima donnas and castrati ruled in the opera house. In the classical style, singers could improvise all they wanted in their arias, embellishing and embroidering the melodies to their hearts' content. There are reports of Rossini attending his own operas and not recognizing some of the arias because of the singers' embellishments and embroidery. Singers often carried with them favorite arias that best showed off their voices, inserting them into the opera of the moment whether they were appropriate or not. Prima donnas were known to physically attack one another — and the composer — if one had more notes in her aria than the other. It was opera forms such as these that led Wagner to agree with Rossini that opera had deteriorated to such an extent that all attempts at drama had been swept away in the showy virtuosity of the performers. Both Wagner and Rossini determined to change this.

Castrati voices appealed to Rossini; many of his roles were sung by these unusual but beautiful voices. In Weinstock's biography, *Rossini*, he reports that Rossini himself narrowly escaped the knife. As a teenager, he had a beautiful boy soprano voice, and there was much discussion among his family as to whether he should become a castrato to preserve his voice and thus ensure an income for his poor family. His mother flatly rejected this proposal. Rossini said of this near-miss, "Would you believe that I came within a hair's breath of belonging to that famous corporation — let us rather say decorporation."

Although Rossini inherited a style of opera that had become stagnant and formalized, one that was at the mercy of the vicissitudes of prima donnas and castrati (tenors were of little importance at the time), he managed, over the course of his short career, to free opera from these limitations, evolving *opera buffa* and *seria* styles into *bel canto*, beautiful singing. He wrote out the embellishments, thus limiting the improvisation of the singers. Rossini was the connection between Gluck, Mozart, and the 18th-century composers, and the grand opera of the 19th-century. The three leading *bel canto* composers were: Rossini, followed by Bellini (*Norma, La Sonnambula*) and Donizetti (*Lucia di Lammermoor, Don Pasquale, L'Elisir d'amore*).

Rossini was born 1792 in Pesaro, a small town on the northern Adriatic coast. Though poor, his father was the town trumpeter and horn player in opera orchestras, and his mother, Anna, was a singer with no training but a beautiful voice. While Rossini was a young child, his parents toured the small opera houses of Italy. For most of Rossini's life, Italy was in a state of war and unrest. Pesaro was a church state under the rule of Rome and the Pope at the time of Rossini's birth. During his lifetime, Napoleonic forces invaded Italy, and French rule alternated with Austrian domination. The once-great music conservatories suffered as a result. Most struggled to survive with poor teachers; there were few good, upcoming composers or singers.

Rossini was a naughty child full of pranks; he would be called hyperactive today. When he got into trouble at school, he would be punished by being sent to pump the bellows at the local smithy's. From his earliest years he studied voice and music with local teachers. When he was ten, his mother's voice gave out and Gioacchino had to start supporting his parents. In 1805, the family moved to Bologna, the center of Italian musical life. This gave the thirteen-year-old Rossini the opportunity to sing and play the harpsicord in church and at the opera for a little money. At fourteen, he was accepted to the prestigious Academia, where the fourteen-year-old Mozart had studied 36 years earlier. At the Academia he absorbed himself in the music of Haydn.

In 1810, the director of a theatre in Venice suddenly found he needed a one-act opera at short notice. Rossini was recommended to him and given his first chance. He was handed a text called *La Cambiale di Matrimonio,* and in a few days had composed the score. The musicians disliked the difficult music and the singers the difficult lines. Rossini, needing a success and money for his parents, compromised, made changes, and the opera was successful. He had arrived. With his instinctive gifts of melody and brio, musical farce, *opera buffa* was his forte. He could turn an absurd, nonsensical story into an opera of sparkling brilliance. Not especially interested, as Mozart and others before him, in the development of character, Rossini's strength lay in fast, humorous action and light, musical, thumbnail sketches. The old guard saw him as a threat to their beloved old forms of opera, while the new welcomed Rossini's effervescence and *joie de vivre.*

Now the whirlwind that was to become his life began. His *La pietra del paragone* played at Italy's premier opera house, La Scala, Milan, in 1812 and rocketed the young Rossini to fame. *Tancredi,* an *opera seria,* soon followed at La Fenice in Venice. For *Tancredi,* Rossini borrowed sections of the overture to *La Pietra del paragone* and put them into his new opera. He had little compunction about taking an overture from a *buffa* opera, changing the tempo, and presenting it in a *seria* work — common practice in his day. Plagiarism, however, became an issue when Rossini wanted to set *The Barber of Seville* to music. Paisiello had written a much-loved *Barber* opera in 1782; his followers were incensed that Rossini had the temerity to challenge the master. Rossini later wrote to the aging Paisiello and said he did not want to enter into a contest with him, but wanted only to treat a subject that delighted him.

Rossini was handed the libretto of *The Barber of Seville* on January 18, 1816 and he delivered the 600-page score to the theatre management on February 6 — three weeks later! The première, held in Rome, was chaotic, for the supporters of Paisiello were determined to sabotage the performance, and a series of accidents didn't help. But Verdi later said of the opera, "I cannot help believing *The Barber of Seville,* for abundance of ideas, for comic verve, and for truth of declamation, the most beautiful *opera buffa* in existence." It is true that Rossini's *Barber* replaced the *Barber* of Paisiello, even as the *Otello* of Verdi later eclipsed the *Otello* written by Rossini.

La Cenerentola also ran into difficulties from the cabal when it premièred in Rome in 1817. The classicists said Rossini would be the death of opera, while the musical romantics defended him. The classicists said: Rossini has spoiled the true forms of harmony, overwhelming vocal music with instrumental; he replaces poetry with a perpetual battle of musical phrases of all colors, one after the other; he forgets that simplicity is the first element of beauty, that the instrumental is but a support for the voice. The romantics responded: the tempest of notes leaves one breathless, the entire family of the noisy instruments assaults, transports, and intoxicates one. For Rossini, the production of operas was a way of living: composed in haste in order to survive, and always with the pleasure of his audience in mind.

Ermione was produced in 1819, when Andrea Leone Tottola based his libretto on Racine's play *Andromaque.* Tottola turned out hundreds of libretti in his lifetime; libretti for which he was paid less than $30 each. Given this, it is not surprising that the quality of the poetry was less than great.

Where Racine's play focuses on Andromaca, Tottola and Rossini decided to make Ermione the central character. Both the play and opera are set in 450 B.C. in Epirus at the end of the Trojan War. Two of The Santa Fe Opera's productions in the 2000 season are from plays set in ancient Greece, with Orestes a common denominator. *Ermione* will not, however, be presented in 450 B.C. Director Jonathan Miller brings *Ermione* into the 19th century in a one-set darkened house. Rossini's music and this story of obsessive love and hatred are timeless, so time and place can be changed in production.

The four protagonists of the story are Ermione, Andromaca, Pirro, and Orestes. Pirro, King of Epirus, is engaged to Ermione, Princess of Greece, but he loves the captive Trojan princess, Andromaca. Orestes, son of the victorious Agamemnon (the king slaughtered by his wife in *Elektra*), loves Ermione but is rejected by her. This is the situation at the start of the opera. Following the Overture, in which the Trojan captives mourn the loss of Troy, Andromaca comes to visit her son, Astyanax. The child is held hostage by Pirro, who allows the mother one hour a day with her child until she consents to become his wife. Andromaca, in her first and only aria, reaffirms her love for her dead husband, Hector, and spurns Pirro's advances. The people of Epirus, represented by Fenicio, Pirro's counselor, cannot encourage the match — if the King marries the daughter of the vanquished Trojan royal family, war could start all over again.

Ermione, in her first entrance, is angry and jealous, insulted by Pirro's love for his captive. At Pirro's arrival the two are mutually scornful and defiant. She threatens, "I will have vengeance." Pirro stands his ground: "Do your worst." Orestes, son of Agamemnon and ambassador from Greece, is announced. He is counseled by his friend, Pilade, to remember that he is on a sacred mission from the Greek kings; but Orestes, in love with Ermione, wants only to be with her.

Before the assembled court, Orestes demands of Pirro that Astyanax, Andromaca's son, be handed over to the Greeks to die, for the Greeks fear that when he grows, "He may become the avenger of his father's death, so that Troy will be born once again from its ruins." Pirro, acting from purely selfish motives, tells Orestes that he will not hand over the child. He publicly announces his love of Andromaca and his desire to marry her, and suggests that Astyanax may "share the throne with me." As the insulted Ermione fumes, Pirro asks Andromaca to marry him, but she refuses. In defiance, Pirro now tells Ermione he has changed his mind, and will marry her (since Andromaca will not have him) and hand over the child to the Greeks.

In a magnificent finale to the first act, the nine soloists express their mixed feelings: Pirro his anger at Andromaca, her determination to resist him, Orestes' love for Ermione, her frustration at Pirro's treatment of her, and Pilade's concern for Orestes. Cleone befriends Ermione, Cefisa befriends Andromaca, while Fenecio and Attalo express their concern at Pirro's actions. When the furious Pirro demands that Astyanax be brought in and handed over to Orestes, Andromaca has second thoughts and agrees to marry Pirro, saying, in an aside, that as soon as the wedding vows are made and Pirro has sworn to protect Astyanax, she will kill herself. Pirro, now jubilant, takes back the child. Ermione approaches madness in her fury, while Pilade attempts to draw Orestes away from the confrontation.

Most of the second act focuses on Ermione's *Gran Scena,* in which her conflicting emotions are expressed — her love for Pirro, her desire for his death, her lust for vengeance. Her love turns to fury as the wedding march of her rival is heard. Handing Orestes a dagger, she asks him to avenge her: "If you love me, go bury this dagger in the heart of my faithless lover." Orestes is appalled, but, out of love, agrees to do her will. As Ermione waits, her thoughts and feelings are confused. "I still do not know whether I love or hate him." Orestes returns with the bloodied dagger and tells her how, once the crown was placed on Andromaca's head, Pirro swore to make her son his heir. This was too much for the men of Epirus, who turned on their king and killed him "with one common cry, 'Vengeance'." Ermione furiously curses Orestes for not listening to her: "What you heard was the voice of a woman in love, maddened and delirious." Orestes realizes the horror of his situation. In an ignoble act, a cowardly assassination, he has killed a king for a woman who does not love him. In the final, fast moments of the opera, Pilade forcibly pulls Orestes away to the waiting Greek ships as Ermione falls senseless to the ground.

This tempestuous plot — a chain of obstructed passions — finds resolution, predictably enough, in tragedy. The protagonists, all royalty, play a deadly game, not for the good of their respective states but for their own personal needs. This is not a noble story of the subordination of passion to duty and honor; the four protagonists are victims of their selfish loves and hatreds for one another. *Ermione* is about obsession and primitive passions simmering just below the surface.

Rossini takes this plot and, with a new awareness of tragedy, molds it within the *opera seria* form. The character of Ermione is fully explored; her emotions, growth, and despair are followed and interpreted in every measure of her music. Though based on a French play, this opera is Italian in its musical form and structure. The Overture, in itself a departure for Rossini, begins *fortissimo* as an offstage men's chorus laments the fall of Troy. Tension builds as Rossini blends memories of the past with furious orchestral reminders of the present. The audience is drawn into the drama from the start. Andromaca's aria virtually grows out of the introduction. In *Ermione*, Rossini moves away from the traditional set numbers for his soloists and ensembles.

Arias, as we know them today, were not common in the early19th-century; in their place were the *cavatina* and *cabaletta*. A *cavatina* is a slow, melodious, lyric song designed to show off the singer's voice and phrasing in terms of tone, nuance, and color. This is followed by the *cabaletta,* or *allegro*, a fast section that demonstrates virtuosity. *Bel canto* singers had to have flawless techniques, pure tone, and an ability to tastefully embellish and decorate the music.

In another departure from the accepted style of his day, Rossini rarely has his soloists sing the same music in the duets and ensembles. As Andromaca and Pirro meet near the beginning, she sings touchingly of her dead husband, while Pirro reveals self-righteousness and bombast in his vocal line. In the stormy *cabaletta* at the end of the duet, Andromaca vows never to wed Pirro. In Pirro's duet with Ermione, the two match one another in arrogance and self-pity. In the music they mirror each other's unhappiness. Their duet ends in a *cabaletta* of breathless fragments: "How can my suffering heart bear such barbarous tortures and yet live?"

The arias for the two men are vastly contrasted. Pirro expresses pride and defiance in a coloratura aria that ranges over two octaves. Orestes' *cavatina* is sweet and heartfelt. His impetuosity and enthusiasm are expressed in orchestral shifts from *forte* to *piano*. This role requires a tenor with a high register; the music for the *cavatina* and *cabaletta* is high and florid, supported by piccolo and clarinet solos.

The first-act finale is sung by nine solo voices to an expressive and simple melody that is taken up by the soloists alternately, then all together. Ermione's *Gran Scena* takes her through three sections of contrasting emotions. As a supplicant, she begs Fenecio to tell Pirro of her love. In a flight of coloratura, she sings of her longing. In the second section, her hopes are destroyed as she hears the wedding march. In the third, she is reduced to fragmented melody as her anger and frustration build to a crescendo. In an extended recitative, accompanied by the full orchestra, Ermione bids Orestes to kill Pirro. When he describes the murder, accompanied by agitated pizzicato strings and wind chords, the music shifts from key to key, reflecting his uncertainty. The opera ends as Orestes and Ermione invoke the Furies, voices overlapping in a final, forceful figuration.

Melody is supreme in all of Rossini's operas, and nowhere is it as intensely felt and matched to its characters as in *Ermione*. The famous Rossini crescendo, consisting of many repetitions of the same passage, each time at a higher pitch and with fuller orchestration, triggers steadily mounting excitement that is irresistible.

Rossini continued his headlong pace of living for ten more years after *Ermione*. In 1822 he married the famous soprano, Isabella Colbran, for whom he had composed many of his leading roles, including *Ermione*. The couple traveled and lived all over Italy, then in London, finally settling in Paris in 1824. There Rossini spent most of the remainder of his long life. He had composed 39 operas by the age of thirty seven. *Guillame Tell*, a fully fledged romantic opera, was his last. Why Rossini stopped composing is not clear. His health was not good; he was exhausted from the many years of being on the road, composing, staging, and conducting. Now financially independent, he could stop. When Isabella died, he married Olympe Pélissier, a woman who loved and cared for him for the rest of his life. In Paris, Rossini was the toast of the town, hosting musical evenings for the French musical world until his death in 1868 at seventy-seven. Rossini had bridged two worlds. Beethoven told the young composer, "Above all, make a lot of *Barbers*," but *Ermione* stands as testimony to the greatness of Rossini in the more substantive medium of tragedy and *opera seria*.

♪

Bibliography

Gossett, Philip, Rossini Opera Festival Program Notes, Pesaro, 1987.

Grout, D.J. *A Short History of Opera,* Columbia University Press, 1965.

Weinstock, Herbert, *Rossini: A Biography,* Alfred .A .Knopf, New York, 1968.

The Eternal Triangle

Venus and Adonis

Sorrow on love hereafter shall attend: it shall be waited on with jealousy. — Shakespeare

Hans Werner Henze's *Venus and Adonis*, based loosely on the Shakespearian verse romance of the same name, is described as "an opera in one act for dancers and singers." Presented as a play within a play, it focuses on Venus' love for the beautiful Adonis, which enrages her lover, Mars, who kills the boy. In Shakespeare's poem (based, in turn, on the Greek myth), Venus falls in love with Adonis, who, preoccupied with his own dreams, pushes her away. Grasping the bridle of Adonis' stallion, she pulls the young man to the ground, entreating him to love her. Adonis begrudgingly grants her a kiss, then runs off to prepare for the hunt the next day. In the course of the hunt he is killed by a wild boar. A distraught Venus clasps the dead Adonis to her breast, and sees him transformed into an anemone, or wind flower, with blood-red petals. She plucks the flower and places it next to her heart. As she returns to the heavens, Venus vows that henceforth love will:

> *Find sweet beginning but unsavory end,*
> *It shall be fickle, false, and full of fraud,*
> *It shall be sparing, and too full of riot,*
> *It shall suspect where is no cause of fear,*
> *It shall be cause of war and dire events.*
> *Since in his prime Death doth my love destroy,*
> *They that love best their loves shall not enjoy.*

While in Shakespeare's poem Mars is mentioned only in passing, Henze and his librettist, Hans-Ulrich Treichel, developed the role and changed the ending.

This opera is about the destructive power of jealousy. In the eternal triangle, the older man loses his beloved to a younger man, whom he then kills. At the death of the boy, the older man realizes that he also loved him. This scenario is played out twice — simultaneously — in *Venus and Adonis*. Three actor-singers come together to read the mythical drama. The older man, called Hero-Player, lives with and loves the Prima Donna. He loses her to Clemente, the young man who reads the part of Adonis. Hero-

Player reads Mars, the god of war, who loves Venus, read by the Prima Donna. Three dancers enact the parts of the three principals as the actors read. The love triangle of myth is mirrored in the real-life triangle of the actor singers. The actors talk, argue, and interact as people do when waiting to read their parts. When they take on the voices of Venus, Adonis, and Mars, the dancers come to life and the parallel lines of the story begin to connect, interact, and move toward tragic resolution. The line between reality and fantasy blurs, and finally disappears when Hero-Player kills Clemente just as the wild boar gores Adonis. The young actor and Adonis, his dream self, die. In Henze's ending (a Straussian one), Adonis becomes a star close to Venus in the firmament. In the heavens his beauty will last forever, the pain and confusion of life left behind as he "Tastes the icy air, [his] mouth filled with dew, [his] tongue a leaf . . . a star amongst stars."

The object of beauty in myth, poem, and opera is Adonis. The woman with whom both men — all men — fall in love is Venus, a diva, the Prima Donna. Hero-Player (Mars) is an aging man who uses all the weapons at his disposal to protect his love and, in using them, destroys forever all he fought to keep. Is the tragic hero of the opera Hero-Player? Perhaps the tragedy is his, for he is left alive and alone, mourning the loss of both the beloved and the boy.

Dreams thread their way through the work. The Prima Donna dreams of the boy as a small dragon with sharp claws and a red tongue. In a somewhat sado-masochistic manner, she longs to capture and smother him with her desire. "You'll suffocate him," Mars tells her. Her love is lustful, predatory and vengeful. (In fairness to Venus, in the original myth she fell for Adonis because she was a victim of one of Cupid's arrows and was powerless to act otherwise.) The curse she places on love at the death of Adonis has been played out over and over again through the centuries. Love comes with a price on its head: death for Clemente/Adonis;

loneliness, alienation, and despair for the Prima Donna/Venus and for Hero-Player/Mars.

The cast of *Venus and Adonis* has three principal singers: The Prima Donna/Venus, a soprano; Hero-Player/Mars, a baritone; and Clemente/Adonis, a tenor. Three dancers mime Venus, Mars, and Adonis, and three more dance the stallion, the mare, and the boar. Six Madrigalists, or shepherds, comment on the action.

The orchestration, with its many changing moods and styles, is the work of a master. Made up of some sixty players, the orchestra is divided into three sections: the Venus section, with flutes, trombones, a harp, and percussion; the Adonis section, with oboes, horns, a celesta, and light percussion; and the Mars section, with clarinets, trumpets, and a piano. Each orchestra has a string section of eleven players. When one character is alone on stage, only that orchestra is heard. "When all three appear together, all three orchestras play at once, each with its own music." (Henze)

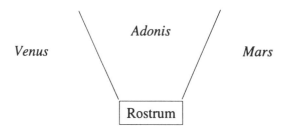

As one critic said, "The music gives access to the opera with its color-rich instrumentation; its late-Romantic sound, its constant boleros rising in a crescendo to Adonis' death; its madrigals rich in *melisma*." The work is a series of scenes set around a suite of boleros. The setting is a rehearsal space. The Prima Donna and Hero-Player, dressed in formal evening dress, sit in the foreground with the lifeless dolls of Venus and Mars on their laps. The center of the stage is reserved for the dancers, who act out the drama in dance.

The opera opens with a sinfonia, or overture, that describes Adonis in beautiful wind solos disrupted by angry brass from the Mars section.

1 Madrigal I The shepherds, in a gentle, ethereal hymn to nature and the dawn, describe the awakening morning. Madrigal form, perfected by Monteverdi in the 17th-century, uses four to six voices to paint words and moods in music using specific harmonic and rhythmic techniques. Henze, referring back to the earlier form, writes brilliantly for the six-part songs. The shepherds sing *a cappella*; their sound suggests trembling as the earth hovers on the verge of day. They sing of Adonis, "the anemone already flowers delicate and pure, the world is filled with sound." The madrigal leads into a beautiful string passage in which the strings from all three sections play together.

2 Recitative I The actors, Hero-Player and the Prima Donna, who are lovers, talk together of their dreams. Hero-Player dreamt his mouth was full of sand; his teeth rolled out, and the Prima Donna, smiling, picked them up and placed them between her lips. In her dream, a small green dragon with sharp claws and a long red tongue perches on her breast. The couple spar sarcastically with one another. The Prima Donna is bored with him; he still loves her and longs for her affection. An icy silence descends as their conversation ends.

3 Bolero I Now the dancers, Venus and Mars, awaken. Venus dances her love for Adonis, while Mars expresses his anger, mistrust, and passion for Venus. Adonis, the dancer, appears hand-in-hand with Clemente, the tenor. While Adonis dances alone, wrapped up in himself, Clemente bows to the Prima Donna and Hero-Player and takes his place beside them. Clemente, the Prima Donna, and Hero-Player read from their black-bound scripts. Clemente tells of Adonis, the innocent who, like Parsifal, dreams only of the hunt, of sleeping in the sun, of watching the clouds roll by, "free from desire." The Prima Donna, reading from her book as Venus, describes the beauty of Adonis and her desire for him; Hero-Player, as Mars, tells of his physical desire for Venus. The bolero, a dance in three time based on the original Basque form, is colorful with exciting percussion rhythms. Each bolero leads to a dance song in which the singers and dancers perform simultaneously.

4 Madrigal II In a clear contrast, the shepherds tell of Adonis' fearlessness and vanity, "impetuous, young, still without fear and in love with the play of his shadow. Like an immortal, he walks through the rising dawn."

5 Bolero II The dancers, Mars and Adonis, practice hunting and war games as Hero-Player and Clemente sing from their books. Mars will teach Adonis how to be brave. They talk of cowardice and death. Mars will forge arms, a golden shield and a suit of armor for the boy. Intriguing string effects intertwine the mixed feelings of the older man with the innocent enthusiasm of Adonis. They sing resolutely, "We shall both vanquish or fall!" then repeat the line hesitantly, uncertainly. Adonis is suddenly overcome with emotion as Mars leaves and Venus enters, approaches the boy, and attempts to caress him. Angrily, he pushes her away and runs offstage. At the same time, mirroring the action of the dancers, the Prima Donna turns to the young tenor, Clemente, and tries to kiss him. He, too, pushes her away and runs off.

6 Recitative II In this near-aria, the Prima Donna compares Clemente to the small dragon of her dream. In a somewhat sadistic manner, she dreams of capturing him and making a real man of him.

7 Bolero III Venus, in her dance, echoes the feelings of the Prima Donna: her hurt, disappointment, frustrated desire, and longing. To the lyrical waltz time of the bolero, the Prima Donna, reading from her book once more, sings of Venus' yearning.

8 Recitative III Hero-Player and the Prima Donna now argue over Clemente. She talks of the "wondrous confusion" of her love;

he demands reason. Hero-Player tells her she will destroy Clemente. They reach no conclusion.

9 Bolero IV   The Prima Donna and Hero-Player read from their books: Mars wants Venus, she only wants Adonis. Together they sing of annihilation: "Perhaps soon will go up in smoke, and wind, and flames, that which was love." The percussive rhythms of the Spanish bolero underscore the intensity of this duet, then die down as singers and dancers leave the stage.

10 Madrigal III   The shepherds, in a song that recalls Monteverdi, sing of nature, the wind, the leaves, the dew. This madrigal, no longer sung *a cappella*, is lightly scored. Adonis enters leading his stallion.

11 Recitative IV   Adonis dreams of Venus. Becoming restive, he gets up and dances. Clemente sings Adonis' thoughts: regretting his rejection of the Prima Donna/Venus, he resolves to return her love. The strings describe his feelings of awakening.

12 Bolero V   Clemente reads Adonis' longing for Venus: "I want to dream and rest, to lie beside you." The sun is now high in the sky; it is noon. Adonis lies in the shade of the tree.

13 Madrigal IV   This lovely, lyrical madrigal, underscored by woodwinds and double basses, describes the lassitude that brings sleep and dreams in the heat of the day.

14 Bolero VI   A mare appears in the clearing; the stallion, scenting her, breaks free of his tether and sets off in pursuit. The horses find each other and flee as Adonis wakes and gives chase. The madrigalists describe the scene with the horses: "First a tender playfulness, then a passionate violent pursuit, through thicket and trees." This is the closest the librettist comes to Shakespeare, who graphically describes, at some length, the coming together of the horses,

He sees his love and nothing else he sees,
He looks upon his love and neighs unto her;

She answers him as if she knew his mind;
As they were mad, unto the wood they hie them.

Adonis, unable to catch them, falls to the ground exhausted as Mars enters, picks him up, and carries him off.

15 Recitative V   Hero-Player and Clemente, the actors, argue over the Prima Donna. Hero-Player says Clemente has fallen into a woman's trap; Clemente defends his love. Hero-Player, goaded to fury, attempts to hit the younger man when he is accused of being jealous. Left alone, he sings of his anger and despair in which he "is alone, everything lost, a raging, helpless creature mocked by his own heartbeat."

16 Bolero VII   Adonis, awakened by Venus, responds at last to her embrace, as the Prima Donna takes Clemente in her arms. In a trio that is a love duet with Mars furiously looking on, the lovers talk of dreams becoming real as they kiss. Hero-Player, unable to stand by any longer, runs forward and stabs Clemente as lightning strikes and the dancing figure of Adonis falls, fatally wounded by the wild boar.

17 Lament for the Dead and Epilogue   The madrigalists and the actor-singers combine to describe the death of Adonis. The Prima Donna/Venus, wild in her grief, sings, "I wish nothing but to go with him, across the river, to where there is silence, dust, night." Hero-Player/Mars realizes remorse: "He, who carried a whole universe of sound on his breath, dead. Could he yet hear me, I would beg him for forgiveness." The great drum roll of death starts the despairing lament, which gradually dies away. The stage darkens and the shepherds turn toward Adonis, who is seen high above them amongst the stars. The music for this transformation is extraordinarily affecting, otherworldly and peaceful. Adonis, close to Venus, assures the madrigalists that, as "A star amongst the stars" he has found peace and is no longer lonely.

Henze described the creation of the opera as "a summation of random daily occurrences, encounters with reality, and the emotions of a rapidly aging old man." When in Spain in the early 1990s, he was attracted to the bolero, a dance not unlike the polonaise, and quite different from the foot-stamping and castanets of flamenco. For Henze, the bolero had "its own distinctive charisma, calm and ceremonial, restrained and austere. This was the classical Basque bolero, a Celtic dance." He was drawn to the "marionette-like charm and stylized grace of the bolero." He conceived a "dance drama performed like an ancient ritual between Venus, Adonis, and Mars." The bolero dancers were to be "outer husks and masks of Venus, Adonis, and Mars, the two horses and the boar." He saw Venus as "an ice-cold, white, glittering star", "the planet Mars as reddish gold, as though on fire"; while "Adonis, by contrast, exists only in the mind." In composition, Henze focused on the style, sound, and form of the opera "unceasingly and obsessively." He says it is necessary for the composer to "live the drama of his characters, experience the jealousy for himself, and suffer the complications of this eternal triangle."

The music of *Venus and Adonis* ranges from elegiac madrigals in the style of Monteverdi, to dialogues or recitatives in the harshly realistic style of Alban Berg. Henze said his three greatest influences were Monteverdi, Mozart, and Mahler, for "their sense of musical realism. These three make the sound of nature sound like the nature of the human soul. The sounds make a strong link between the landscape and the listener's mind."

Hans Werner Henze has lived through turbulent times. Born in Gütersloh in northern Germany in 1926, his childhood was fractured by the advent of Nazism. His father became an ardent Nazi; young Hans was required to join the Hitler Youth. He fought for Germany in World War II, was captured by the British, and became a prisoner-of war. At the end of hostilities he returned home and resumed his music studies under Wolfgang Fortner, moving on to study serialism with René Leibowitz. One of his early loves was ballet; he was the artistic director of the Staatstheater Ballet in Wiesbaden in the early 1950s. His collaboration with the *doyen* of British ballet, Frederick Ashton, led to his composition of the ballet *Ondine* in 1958. Margot Fonteyn's interpretation of the water sprite rocketed the ballet to fame. (One of the greatest theatre experiences of my life was *Ondine* in the sixties, with Fonteyn dancing to Henze's music at Covent Garden.) Henze, by this time, had fused his early neo-classical style with serialism. In reaction to Nazism and fascism, he became committed to the New Left, socialism, and communism in the late 1960s. This shift had a major effect on his music. Where his early works were drawn from classical texts that expressed themes of isolation and alienation, now he turned to politically radical texts. He moved from Germany to Italy in 1953 and has lived there ever since. Italy brought color and richness to his work. Henze says of his music, "the old forms strive to regain significance, even when the modern timbre of the music seldom or never allows them to appear on the surface." He founded the music festival at Montepulciano in 1976, and the Munich International Festival of New Music in 1988.

Henze has an enormous following in Germany; he is unquestionably one of the great composers of the late 20th-century. John Crosby must be thanked for presenting the American premières of his operas at The Santa Fe Opera: *The Stag King* in 1965; *Boulevard Solitude* in 1967 (this opera, Henze's first, was a new telling of the story of Manon Lescaut). *The Bassarids*, in 1968 (based on Euripides' *The Bacchae*, with a libretto by W.H. Auden and Chester Kallman); *We Come to the River* (an attack on militarism and materialism) in 1984; and *The English Cat,* (a Victorian comedy of manners) in 1985. The première of both *Venus and Adonis* and his Ninth Symphony occurred after Henze's

70th-birthday, in 1997. *Venus and Adonis* was an enormous success at its first performance, at the Munich Staatsoper on 11 January 1997; a concert performance followed later that year as part of The BBC Promenade Concerts at the Royal Albert Hall in London. The Santa Fe Opera presents the American première in 2000.

Venus and Adonis has been described by critics as "unconstrainedly romantic, [but it is] also trim and sure. Its musical world is Henze's own; Monteverdi and Alban Berg have helped to shape it." Henze fuses many worlds in *Venus and Adonis*: in the linking of ancient myth and Shakespeare with a contemporary libretto, in the superimposing of one drama over another, and in the musical styles that range from the madrigals of Monteverdi to the realism of Alban Berg. Toward the end of a long musical career, Henze has provided a stimulating work that demonstrates his mastery of orchestration in a challenging scenario.

♪

Bibliography

Henze, Hans Werner, *Music and Politics: Collected Writings 1953-81,* Faber and Faber Ltd., London, 1982.

Henze, Hans Werner, *Bohemian Fifths, An Autobiography*, Princeton University Press, 1999.

Program Notes, BBC Proms 1997, Royal Albert Hall, London, 1997.

Program Notes, The Santa Fe Opera, 1965 and 1984.

Shakespeare, William, "Venus and Adonis," Collins, London, 1954.